Practical Debugging in C++

Ann R. Ford • Toby J. Teorey • Gary S. Tyson

Dear Team,
In times of uncertainty and
darkness, here is something to get
you back on track.

Best wishes,
JM

Cover photograph courtesy of Frank Greenaway/Dorling Kindersley.

Previously published as:

Practical Debugging in C++ ™
by Ann R. Ford, Toby J. Teorey, Gary S. Tyson

Published by Prentice Hall

Printed in the United States of America

10 9 8 7 6 5 4 3 2 1

ISBN 0-536-98765-3

2005200049

EC/SM

Please visit our web site at *www.pearsoncustom.com*

PEARSON CUSTOM PUBLISHING
75 Arlington Street, Suite 300, Boston, MA 02116
A Pearson Education Company

Contents

Preface

This book is a tutorial on debugging techniques for both the beginning and intermediate programmer. For the beginning programmer it is meant to be a companion book to any introduction to programming in C++. Ideally this book is for student to take it to their computer labs with them for quick reference when writing and debugging C++ programs. For the intermediate programmer, particularly those with some experience in other languages, this guide provides a quick up-to-speed primer in C++ debugging with a series of examples of common syntax and semantic errors and how they can be detected and corrected.

The motivation for this book came as a result of innumerable sessions in the computer lab with introductory programming classes. Unfortunately, many beginning programmers subscribe to the "programming by blind faith" method, writing the complete program, then hoping it will run correctly the first time without doing any intermediate testing, and then panicking when it crashes or generates bad data that cannot be explained. Each time they come to us with "What do I do now?" we go back to the program together to look over the basic logic, and then start inserting traces to check the intermediate results and localize the sources of error. We have come to the conclusion that students need a short, clear debugging guide as a valuable addition to their programming tools, something they can easily carry with them and with which they can supplement their introductory programming textbooks.

First we describe the most common syntactic and semantic programming errors, with illustrative examples, and explains how to correct them. Then we show the student how to use output statements (cout) to trace variables in C++ programs using classes, and how tracing can be easily inserted into his or her own programs. Several examples are given to illustrate how tracing can help find bugs - especially when a program runs without any runtime errors, but the results are incorrect. It also is useful to find errors quickly when the program crashes with an error message or just hangs up, leaving the programmer with no option but to kill the program and reboot the computer, over and over, until the bug is found.

Finally we illustrate how to use a debugger effectively. Most compilers come with debuggers now, and students need to be able to use them at some point during their first course in programming. We strongly recommend learning to use both tracing and the debugger as alternative approaches.

The appendices give a summary of the most common bugs found in first C++ programs and a checklist of techniques for error detection and prevention. The examples in this book conform to the 1999 ISO/ANSI C++ standard.

Who should read this book?

Beginning programmers will like this book because it is a quick read with many simple examples, both numeric and non-numeric. It should save them many frustrating hours of debugging time when they apply the tracing and system debugger techniques illustrated in Chapters 3 to 5. Furthermore, anyone using this book can easily read any chapter independently of the others. This should also appeal to the more experienced programmers who want to review their knowledge of debugging without wading through all the fundamentals. Instructors in introductory programming classes may want to recommend this book to their students because it will make them much more self-sufficient, and it will greatly reduce the time they need for individual counseling for their programs.

How to use this book.

Beginning programmers should peruse Chapters 1 and 2 to get a quick overview of the basic types of errors programmers tend to make. Chapters 3 and 4 are self-contained discussions of how to use tracing in your programs with the minimum of effort. Chapter 5 is more advanced and may be used later, when you feel the need for more debugging options, especially for larger programs.

Acknowledgments

We wish to acknowledge the excellent critiques of this book by Tim Budd, Guillermo Francia III, Aaron J. Marks, Paul McNamee, Neil C. Obremski, and George Policello.

CHAPTER 1

Introduction

1.1 CHAPTER OBJECTIVES

- To motivate the programmer to learn and use debugging skills from the start
- To understand what types of errors occur in programs
- To learn what types of debugging tools and techniques are generally available to find and correct these different types of errors

1.2 MOTIVATION FOR DEBUGGING SKILLS

We all have read numerous stories of the results of poor programming, from banking errors that result in loss (or gain) of funds for no apparent reason, to medical record mistakes, or spacecraft communication systems that go awry. In some cases serious injury or worse has been caused by public transportation failures or medical equipment failures due to computer software errors. These spectacular problems have led to the rise and importance of professional ethics and responsibility in the computing profession, to try to minimize and eventually remove the sources of errors.

These problems are often the results of errors or "bugs" that were introduced into the software code by the programmer and never detected nor corrected. In order to minimize the errors you get in programs, it is extremely important to learn the skills of good programming early and keep them constantly in mind. A very good reference for good programming design and implementation is the popular book "The Practice of Programming" by Kernighan and Pike (see Kern99).

Good programming skills are learned through hard work and attention to detail. A well-designed program will eliminate many, but not all errors. Program coding will often generate errors, even for a well designed system, and the code will need to be closely checked at all stages of implementation. Compilers, which translate your source code into machine executable code, will check your syntax and generate error messages, so you can quickly find the errors and correct them.

After the syntax errors have been corrected, you are mostly on your own to find so-called "semantic" errors—that is, code that has correct syntax, but still has incorrect logic (meaning) and thus generates errors during program execution. Some of these errors are very hard to detect, so you need to develop special skills to find them. It is the main purpose of this book to give you the skills necessary to find and correct semantic errors. The two most important approaches to correcting semantic errors are tracing using C++ output statements, and using the system interactive debugger. Examples of semantic errors that commonly occur in first programs include using "<" instead of "<=" to decide when to terminate a loop, accessing array elements that go beyond the original array definition, or simply forgetting to initialize your variables.

Many errors that occur during program execution may be due less to program logic than to data values that cause problems. A typical example of such an error occurs when the denominator becomes zero just before a division operation is attempted, and the system generates an error message like "program error: attempted to divide by zero". Another error message could occur when the result of a multiplication or other arithmetic operation generates a value that is too large (or too small) to be adequately represented by the numerical limits of your computer, thus generating a message "program error: numerical overflow (or underflow)". These types of errors can also be detected and corrected with the tracing techniques or use of the debugger that we recommend in this book. They can also be detected and dealt with automatically in object-oriented C++ using exception handling techniques, but this approach is beyond the scope of this book. We refer you to a more advanced textbook in C++ for the details, for example see Deitel and Deitel [Deit05], or Savitch [Savi04].

Some errors are created by bad input data and are not necessarily the fault of the programmer. However, it is still the programmer's duty to include in his or her code, ways to check for bad input data, to generate error messages when bad data is found, and in some cases, to terminate the program execution. This is often referred to as "error checking" code.

1.3 APPROACHES TO DEBUGGING

When semantic or other run-time errors occur, there are three basic approaches you can take to determine what the problem is and how to correct it.

1. Trace by hand

In this approach, you look at a program listing and trace each step of program execution by hand and try to recreate the results of the actual program execution. This is usually a good starting point for error correction, especially for small programs or simple functions. It forces you to think through the program logic in a methodical manner. For large programs this process can be very time consuming, and you may then have to resort to computer-aided (program) tracing.

2. Program tracing

Program tracing (see Chapters 3 and 4) uses tracing (print) statements inserted into programs at key locations to track the changing of variable values so you can see how the program is progressing, step by step. Basic tracing can be done by inserting individual "cout" statements in C++ and using them to specify the location of the trace and current value of all variables. Extended tracing involves the use of flags and function calls to make the tracing easier to turn on and off, and to minimize the amount of code that has to be written and inserted into the program.

3. System interactive debugger

Most programming language environments in use today include a debugger (see Chapter 5), a software package that allows you to run your program in a step by step mode, automatically keeping track of all variables in the program as it executes one step (statement) at a time. You can also set breakpoints which allow the program to run free of tracing overhead to a certain location, and then stop to display all the program variables and their values.

All of these debugging techniques are valuable to understand and use. We recommend that you start with tracing by hand because it forces you to make sure you fully understand the program requirements and what your program logic is doing. When this is no longer giving you any insight about where to locate runtime errors, we recommend the extensive use of program tracing with inserted output (cout) statements. In most programs, this method will find all semantic and other run-time errors and should be sufficient. In some cases, however, you may want to use the system interactive debugger. The choice between program tracing and using the system debugger is often one of personal style, but it is important to know how to use both, so that your choice is an informed one. Now, on with the details of debugging!

CHAPTER 2

Common Syntax and Semantic Errors

2.1 CHAPTER OBJECTIVES

- To understand the fundamental characteristics of syntax and semantic errors
- To be able to identify specific common syntax and semantic errors frequently encountered by beginning programmers
- To be able to interpret a syntax warning
- To be able to apply appropriate techniques to correct these common errors

2.2 SYNTAX ERRORS

A *syntax error* is a violation of the syntax, or grammatical rules, of a natural language or a programming language. The following sentence contains an error of English syntax:

```
I is going to the concert tonight.
```

If we write or say this sentence, other English speakers will know that we have used incorrect grammar, however they will still understand what we *mean*. Programming languages are not so forgiving, however. If we write a line of C++ code containing a syntax error, the compiler does *not* know what we mean. A syntax error is considered a *fatal compilation error*, because the compiler cannot translate a C++ program into executable code if even one syntax error is present.

2.2.1 Syntax Errors: Summary of Important Points

- *How are they detected?* The compiler detects them when you try to compile your program.
- *Why do they occur?* The syntax rules of C++ have been violated.
- *Is there object code generated?* No, so you cannot run the program.
- Solution: find the line(s) which contain syntax error(s) using the compiler's flagged lines and error messages; using your textbook or other C++ reference as a guide, correct them.
- Remember, frequently, a syntax error occurs not in the line flagged by your compiler, but in some line *above* that line; it is often the previous line, but not necessarily.

2.2.2 Examples: Common Syntax Errors

Some syntax errors are very common, especially for beginning programmers, and the examples that follow should help you identify and correct many syntax errors in whatever program you are currently working on. The syntax diagrams in your C++ textbook or a C++ reference book should be your ultimate guide in correcting these types of errors.

Different compilers report syntax errors in different formats. For these examples, we will assume that the compiler displays errors in the following way, for a C++ program named "myprog.cpp" :

```
Syntax Error: <description of error>
Line <line number here> of program myprog.cpp
```

The first line indicates that a syntax error message is being displayed, and then gives a brief description of what the compiler thinks the error is. The second line will give the line number on which the compiler has identified the error.

Compilers that provide a graphical user interface (GUI), using windows and various graphical items to display information for you, may display all such error messages in one window (which we will assume for our discussion here), or they may simply list the program with erroneous lines highlighted or pointed to by an arrow or other graphic, with written error messages shown off to the side. In any event, error messages displayed by different compilers are generally very similar.

An important note about compilers: modern compilers are typically very accurate in identifying syntax errors, and will help you enormously in correcting your code. However, compilers often present two difficult problems for new programmers: (1) they can frequently miss reporting an actual error on one line, but get "thrown off-track," then report errors on subsequent lines which are not truly errors; the compiler may then also display error messages which are incorrect, and (2) after encountering one true syntax error, compilers often generate many syntax error messages; again, the compiler has been "thrown off-track" by a particular error. Why does this occur?

Basically, because a compiler is a very complex and sophisticated language-processing program, and no computer program can analyze any language as well as a human being can at this point in time.

What, then, is your best strategy for eliminating syntax errors?

- display the current list of syntax errors (print it if you like)
- start at the first error listed, try to correct it, and then re-compile your program; sometimes many errors will drop out after one error is fixed
- if you are having trouble with a particular error listed for a specific line, yet you are 100% sure that line is correct, then search for a syntax error in the lines ABOVE that line, starting with the line immediately preceding the line under consideration, and working backwards; usually the actual error will be found in a line close to the line flagged, though not always
- repeat this process until all errors are eliminated

Specific examples follow.

Missing Semicolon In the C++ code that follows, three declarations are given. Line numbers (chosen in all examples arbitrarily) are shown to the left of each line.

```
5 int num;
6 float value
7 double bigNum;
```

A C++ compiler would generate an error something like this:

```
Syntax Error: semicolon expected
Line 6 of program myprog.cpp
```

To fix this error, just add a semicolon after the identifier "value," as in

```
6 float value;
```

Undeclared Variable Name - version 1 If the preceding code were compiled and included an assignment statement as in

```
5 int num;
6 float value
7 double bigNum;
8 bigNum = num + value;
```

we often would see the following additional error message:

```
Syntax Error: undeclared identifier "bigNum"
Line 8 of program myprog.cpp
```

This is a situation in which there is actually no syntax error on the line flagged, and the real error occurs on a line above it. Line 8 is totally correct! If we correct the problem in line 6, the error reported for line 8 will drop out the next time we compile the program.

Undeclared Variable Name - version 2 What about the following?

```
5    int num;
6    float value;
7    double bigNum;
8    bignum = num + value;
```

we would see the following error message:

```
Syntax Error: undeclared identifier "bignum"
Line 8 of program myprog.cpp
```

This is a different problem; in this case, an error actually exists on line 8. The lower case `n` in `bignum` must be changed to an uppercase `N`, or else the variable name does not match its declaration. Remember, in C++ declarations, lowercase letters are different from uppercase letters.

Undeclared Variable Name - version 3 Missing Reference to Namespace
Consider the following program:

```
1    #include <iostream>
2    int main ( )
3    {
4        cout << "Hello World!!!";
5        return 0;
6    }
```

A compiler will generate an error message like this:

```
Syntax Error: undeclared identifier "cout"
Line 4 of program myprog.cpp
```

The problem is that `cout` is defined in a `namespace` named `std`. To correct this error, we need only add the following line, right after line 1 in the preceding program:

```
using namespace std;
```

Unmatched Parentheses Given the code

```
5    result = (firstVal - secondVal / factor;
```

the compiler would generate an error message like

```
Syntax Error: ')' expected
Line 5 of program myprog.cpp
```

We could correct this error with

```
5 result = (firstVal - secondVal) / factor;
```

Note that similar syntax errors can occur with unmatched braces, { and }.

Unterminated Strings It is easy to forget the last double quote in a string, as in

```
21    const string ERROR_MESSAGE = "bad data entered!;
```

or

```
45    cout << "Execution Terminated << endl;
```

Both will provoke the compiler to print something similar to

```
Syntax Error: illegal string constant
```

Both can be fixed by adding the terminating double quote to the string:

```
21    const string ERROR_MESSAGE = "bad data entered!";
```

or

```
45    cout << "Execution Terminated" << endl;
```

Left Hand Side of Assignment does not Contain an L-Value Look at the following statements, where the intent of the assignment statement in line 7 is to calculate `x * y` and store the result in `product`:

```
6 double x = 2.0, y = 3.1415, product;
7 x * y = product;
```

Many C++ compilers will print an error message like

```
Syntax Error: not an l-value
Line 7 of program myprog.cpp
```

But what does this mean? An "l-value" roughly refers to a value which specifies the address of a location in memory, where something can be stored. We can think of it as the Left side of an assignment, and what we know about the syntax of this statement is that the left hand side must contain the name of a *variable*. Nothing else is valid in this position. Therefore, we correct this error using

```
7 product = x * y;
```

Value-Returning Function has no Return Statement A function declared with a return type must contain a return statement. Consider the following function, which is supposed to round its float parameter up or down appropriately:

```
int RoundFloat (float floatToRound)
{
        int roundedValue;
        roundedValue = int (floatToRound + 0.5);
}
```

This function calculates a correct result in the local variable `roundedValue`, but it never returns this result. Some compilers will merely generate a warning message for this function (to be discussed later in this chapter), others will generate a syntax error. In any event, the error can be corrected by adding a `return` statement, as in

```
int RoundFloat (float floatToRound)
{
        int roundedValue;
        roundedValue = int (floatToRound + 0.5);
        return (roundedValue);
}
```

Can't Convert int* to int** (and similar errors) Many times we need to pass an array to a function. Let's suppose we have these declarations:

```
const int NUM_SCORES = 100;
typedef int ScoreList [NUM_SCORES];
void ProcessScores (ScoreList inputScores [NUM_SCORES]);
ScoreList scores;
```

Now let's assume we call the function `ProcessScores` and pass the array variable `scores` like this:

```
10  ProcessScores (scores);
```

A compiler will generate an error message something like

```
Syntax Error: can't convert int* to int**
Line 10 of program myprog.cpp
```

What is wrong here? The data type of the argument `scores`, and the data type of the corresponding parameter `inputScores`, do *not* match. Array `scores` is a one-dimensional array of `int`. In the prototype we have written above, `inputScores` is a two-dimensional array of `int`. The corrected version of the prototype for the function is

```
void ProcessScores (ScoreList inputScores);
```

Remember, the data types of arguments and parameters must generally match in three places—a function's prototype, its heading, and calls to that function. C++ does perform some type conversions automatically, but as part of defensive programming and good style, it is generally not wise to use data types which do not match.

Illegal Function Overloading This is another common error message generated when the data types of arguments and parameters in a function's prototype, its heading, and calls to that function, do not all match. As discussed in the previous example, it is typically best to utilize matching data types in all of these three program elements. Note that this error message may be generated when you are trying to call a C++ library function, as well as when you try to call functions you have written yourself.

2.3 SYNTAX WARNINGS

From the discussion thus far, you know that a syntax *error* is a *fatal compilation error*, that is, the compiler cannot translate your program into executable code. Compilers also can generate syntax *warning* messages, which are not fatal errors, and are often very helpful in the debugging process. A syntax warning is displayed when the compiler has found that the syntax of some part of your code is valid, but it is potentially erroneous anyway. Compiler writers, being programmers themselves, are familiar with common programming errors and usually build some error checking of this type into the compiler. Let's look at a few examples.

2.3.1 Syntax Warnings: Summary of Important Points

- *How are they detected?* The compiler detects them when you compile your program

- *Why do they occur?* The syntax rules of C++ have *not* been violated, but the compiler writers have built in special error checking for certain common programming errors, and the compiler has found a possible error of this type
- *Is there object code generated?* Yes, so you can run the program
- Solution: Find the line(s) containing the syntax warning(s), and check them very carefully to see if you think they do contain true errors
- Remember, a syntax warning should *always* be taken seriously, because there is probably a real error in your code if the compiler issues a warning message

2.3.2 Examples: Common Syntax Warnings

Using "=" when "==" is Intended Given this `if` statement,

```
20   if (num = 100)
21        cout << "num equals 100";
22   else
23        cout << "num is not 100";
```

many compilers would display something like the following warning message:

```
Syntax Warning: assignment operator used in if expression
Line 20 of program myprog.cpp
```

What is the problem with this code? You may have noticed that the equal sign used in the `if` expression is actually an assignment operator, not the relational operator, which tests for equality. In this code, `num` is set to 100 because of the assignment, and the expression `num = 100` is *always* true, because the value of the expression is actually 100. The corrected code for this example would be

```
20   if (num == 100)
```

Loop has no Body Consider the following `for` loop, which is supposed to print out the numbers between 1 and 10, along with their squares:

```
int lcv;
for (lcv = 1; lcv <= 10; lcv++);
cout << lcv << "    " << lcv * lcv
      << endl;
```

This loop, if run, would print only

```
11   121
```

When we try to compile this loop, a good compiler would generate the following warning message:

```
Syntax Warning: for loop has no body
Line 10 of program myprog.cpp
```

We would correct this code by removing the erroneous semicolon, as follows:

```
10    for (int lcv = 1; lcv <= 10; lcv++)
```

Uninitialized Variable Consider the following code, which is supposed to read characters until the user hits `return`:

```
10    char ch;
11    while (ch != '\n')
12          cin >> ch;
```

When we try to compile this version, many compilers would generate the following warning message:

```
Syntax Warning: variable "ch" is uninitialized
Line 11 of program myprog.cpp
```

In this code, the variable `ch` is tested for a value when it has not received a value yet. This code as it is, will not execute correctly. We can fix this problem using a priming read, as follows:

```
10    char ch;
11    cin >> ch;
12    while (ch != '\n')
13          cin >> ch;
```

All of the errors discussed here which generate warning messages are what we call *semantic* errors, to be discussed in the next section.

To illustrate what we have looked at so far in this chapter, Figure 2.1 shows a portion of the syntax errors and warnings window generated by the Metrowerks CodeWarrior Development Studio for Windows, version 9, for a specific program. Looking at this figure, notice in particular how errors and warnings are flagged with different graphics elements. Figure 2.2 shows the window generated by the Microsoft Visual C++ 6.0 compiler for the same program. If you click, double-click, or right click on the line describing a syntax error, you will typically see more information depending on which compiler you are using. Notice how these two compilers produce similar, but not identical, error reports. Other compilers will also produce similar error and warning messages.

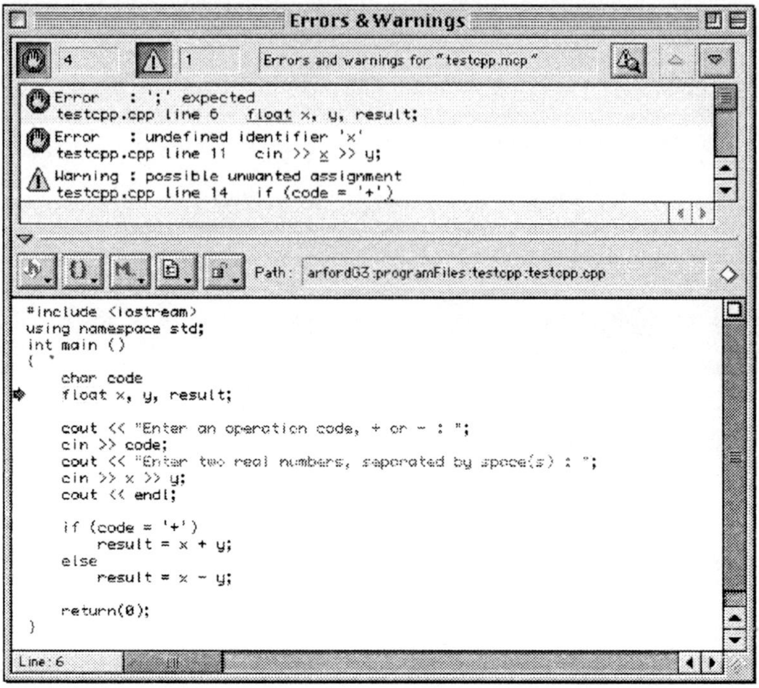

Figure 2.1

Example Program in Metrowerks Code Warrior Syntax Errors and Warnings Windows

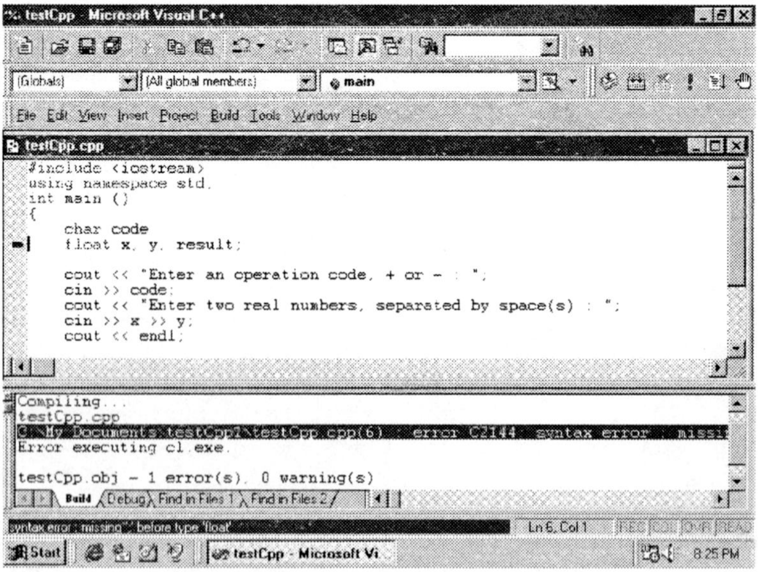

Figure 2.2

Example Program in Microsoft Visual C++ Syntax Errors and Warnings Windows

2.4 SEMANTIC ERRORS

A *semantic error* is a violation of the rules of *meaning* of a natural language or a programming language. The following sentence contains an error of English semantics:

```
My refrigerator just drove a car to Miami.
```

If we write or say this sentence, other English speakers may begin to wonder about our sanity, but they will nevertheless know that our syntax is perfectly correct! Since a compiler only checks for correct use of syntax, it is not able to evaluate whether or not we have written code whose *meaning* is correct. Semantic errors are much harder to detect and correct than are syntax errors, and they are also more common.

When there are semantic errors in a C++ program, the compiler *does* translate the program into executable code. Most semantic errors do NOT generate compiler warnings. When the program is run, however, it does not work correctly.

2.4.1 Summary of Important Points

- *How are they detected?* Semantic errors usually are detected by the programmer or by a user of a program, often while reading output and finding it is incorrect.
- *Why do they occur?* The syntax rules of C++ have been correctly followed, but the meaning of the code is incorrect (e.g. faulty algorithms, algorithms not translated into C++ correctly, values calculated or input erroneously, flow of control is wrong, etc.).
- *Is there object code generated?* Yes, so you can run the program.
- Solution: Find the line(s) which contain the semantic error(s), using extra print statements, hand tracing or an interactive debugger if needed, and correct them.
- Remember, semantic errors are undoubtedly the most common type of error, and they are the hardest to find and correct, so prevention in the form of good design and defensive programming are often your best tools.

2.4.2 Examples: Common Semantic Errors

Infinite Loop An infinite loop, which repeats indefinitely, is often created when a programmer writes a loop in which the expression tested never becomes false. For example, consider the following code, which is intended to read a lower case 'y' or 'n' from the user:

```
char response;
cout << "Please enter (y)es or (n)o -> ";
cin >> response;
while ((response != 'y') || (response != 'n'))
{
    cout << "Please try again. Enter (y)es or (n)o -> ";
    cin >> response;
}
```

The expression

```
(response != 'y') || response != 'n')
```

is always true, regardless of what input is entered by the user. If the user enters a ‘y’, then the first part of the expression is false, but the second part of the expression is true. Thus the entire expression is true because of the OR operation. Because of this property, the loop is infinite. The following expression is the corrected version, which merely substitutes AND for OR, and is false when the user enters either a ‘y’ or an ‘n’, allowing the loop to exit:

```
(response != 'y') && (response != 'n')
```

Misunderstanding of Operator Precedence Misunderstanding of the operator precedence rules can often lead to expressions which evaluate incorrectly. Consider the following code, which is intended to calculate the miles per gallon achieved by a car:

```
float startMileage,
      endMileage,
      gallonsUsed,
      milesPerGallon;
cout << "Please enter the starting mileage, the ending"
      << " mileage, and the number of gallons used by the"
      << " car -> ";
cin >> startMileage >> endMileage >> gallonsUsed;
milesPerGallon = endMileage - startMileage / gallonsUsed;
```

Since division has higher precedence than subtraction, the final assignment statement evaluates incorrectly. The corrected version is as follows:

```
milesPerGallon = (endMileage - startMileage) / gallonsUsed;
```

Programmers often make liberal use of parentheses to prevent this kind of error in the first place, as part of *defensive programming*.

Dangling Else The "dangling else" is a very common and subtle error in the flow of control of a nested `if` statement. Remember, compilers ignore indentation, and pair an *else* clause with the most recent unmatched *then* clause. The following code is intended to print out the word "both" if the `bool` variables `relative` and `myFriend` are both true, and print out "neither" if both are false.

```
if (relative)
    if (myFriend)
        cout << "both";
else
    cout << "neither";
```

When this code is run, it prints "both" correctly, when both `bool` variables are true. However, if both variables are false, it prints nothing! Further, when `relative` is true but `myFriend` is false, it prints "neither!" There are many ways to fix or rewrite this code, but let's consider one very common correction technique here. The following code forces the compiler to pair the else with the first if, instead of with the second if, and therefore works correctly:

```
if (relative)
{
    if (myFriend)
        cout << "both";
}
else
    cout << "neither";
```

Off-by-One Error The off-by-one error generally describes a loop that iterates one fewer or one more time than is correct. Consider the following code, which is supposed to read in 50 values from the user, and keep a running total:

```
const int NUM_VALUES = 50;
int lcv,
    someValue,
    total = 0;
for (lcv = 1; lcv < NUM_VALUES; lcv++)
{
    cout << "Enter an integer ->";
    cin >> someValue;
    total = total + someValue;
}
```

What happens when this code is executed? The user is prompted 49 times, and 49 values are read in and summed. The following small change in the `for` loop heading fixes this problem:

```
for (lcv = 1; lcv <= NUM_VALUES; lcv++)
```

or, alternatively, we can write

```
for (lcv = 0; lcv < NUM_VALUES; lcv++)
```

Code Inside a Loop That Does Dot Belong There The following code, adapted from the previous example, is intended to read in a series of 50 numbers entered by the user, calculate the running total, and print out both the final total and the average value of all the numbers.

```
const int NUM_VALUES = 50;
int lcv,
        someValue,
        total = 0,
        average;
for (lcv = 1; lcv <= NUM_VALUES; lcv++)
{
        cout << "Enter an integer ->";
        cin >> someValue;
        total = total + someValue;
        average = total / NUM_VALUES;
        cout << "Total is: " << total << endl;
        cout << "Average is: " << average;
}
```

When this code is executed, it produces a disturbing result! The output is very long, because the total and average are both printed out 50 times. Moreover, they are correct only the last time they are printed. What is wrong? The last three lines which are inside the loop do not belong there, they must be placed outside the loop and after it for the code to work correctly. The corrected version of this code is as follows:

```
for (lcv = 1; lcv <= NUM_VALUES; lcv++)
{
    cout << "Enter an integer ->";
    cin >> someValue;
    total = total + someValue;
}
```

```
average = total / NUM_VALUES;
cout << "Total is: " << total << endl;
cout << "Average is: " << average;
```

Not Using a Compound Statement When One is Required The following code is intended to read in a text file and echoprint its contents (for this example, assume that `infile` is the file variable name and the file has just been opened successfully).

```
char ch;
infile.get (ch);
while (infile)          // while input stream has not failed
    cout << ch;         // echoprint the current character
    infile.get (ch);    // read the next character
```

The programmer has indented this code to show that both the `cout` and the `get` calls are inside the loop. However, the compiler interprets it differently. When executed, this code reads one character from the file (assuming the file does contain at least one character), and then enters an infinite loop, printing that same character over and over indefinitely. The following code contains the addition of a compound statement, and thus is correct:

```
infile.get (ch);
while (infile)
{
    cout << ch;         // echoprint the current character
    infile.get (ch);    // read the next character
}
```

Array Index Bounds Error The following code is intended to read in seven temperature values, one for each day of the week, and load them into a seven element array.

```
const int NUM_DAYS = 7;
int temperatures[NUM_DAYS];
int count;
for (count = 1; count <= NUM_DAYS; count++);
{
    cout << "Enter a temperature: ";
    cin >> temperatures [count];
}
```

Let's say that we execute this code as it is written. Many problems may result, because the code contains a fundamental error: the array's correct indices range from 0 through 6, while the array indices used in the `for` loop range from 1 through 7. The array element `temperatures[0]` is never used. The attempt to access an array element with `temperatures[7]` is wrong, because `temperatures[7]` does not exist.

The results of reading in the array with this loop and then attempting to use the array later in the same program are somewhat unpredictable and are partly dependent on what indices are used later on. The program may even *crash* (a *runtime* error). We may find that an error message such as "Bus Error" or "Segmentation Fault" or "Addressing Exception" is printed at the time of the crash. Alternatively, the program may keep running, and the value of count may be overwritten by whatever value the user types in for the last array element, which causes other unpredictable behavior. The fundamental problem is that when invalid array indices are used, a C++ program will access memory locations which are not valid portions of the array. C++ does not prevent such array index errors by performing what is called "bounds checking." To avoid this problem, you must be very careful to write your code so that only valid indices are used. We can correct the code above by using this conventional `for` loop control for such an array:

```
for (count = 0; count < NUM_DAYS; count++);
```

A Final Note

This concludes our introductory discussion of syntax errors and warnings, and semantic errors. While working on your programming assignments on a computer, you may wish to keep this book with you as a helpful guide in determining what exactly the compiler is trying to tell you when you see one of its sometimes obscure error messages. In addition, by studying the examples of all of the common errors described in this chapter, you may be able to prevent many of them from occurring in the first place, as you will have the knowledge and the tools to avoid them altogether.

CHAPTER 3

Tracing Techniques for Debugging

3.1 CHAPTER OBJECTIVES

- To understand the principles of program tracing as an effective debugging tool
- To be able to insert tracing code in your program to find run-time errors
- To quickly identify the location of a run-time error and determine the cause of that error
- To use print tracing of function calls and control statements to better understand the execution flow of a program
- To use print tracing of variables to better understand the data flow of a program

3.2 BASIC TRACING

Print statements are common in all programs; they are used to specify program output, exceptional events and program errors. In this chapter we will show that print tracing in C++ can also be an effective tool in finding semantic and run-time errors. In much the same way as spelunkers find their way back to the opening of the cave by laying out a path of rope to trace their path from its very beginning, carefully placed print statements can identify the execution path taken by the program; this may differ from the expectation of the programmer. They can also illustrate important program data throughout the execution of the program—parameter values, loop indices, expression values, etc.

Tracing using extra print statements is one of the most important methods for debugging computer programs. We will look at several simple examples of how tracing is done and how it can be of incredible benefit to you when the computer crashes or hangs up and you don't have any idea where the error occurred, or when the program runs to completion without any crash or error message, but the output is incorrect. In both cases, you may or may not have a clue as to where the error is occurring, and unlike syntax errors that the compiler catches, you may not have any system messages to help in locating the problem.

Tracing is a method of inserting print statements into your program at key locations to print out (or just display on your screen) the current status (current value) of certain variables in your program so you can see how those values are changing during the execution of the program. You can follow the execution step-by-step if you wish by putting in print statements after every line of source code. However, this would be wasteful of time and energy—your trace can be done better by first carefully selecting where to insert the print statements so that their output will provide you with the maximum amount of useful debugging information.

Before we discuss the placement of print statements, let's first back up and examine the process of debugging in a systematic manner. There are 4 steps involved in debugging any program:

1. Determining that an error exists,
2. Identifying the type of error,
3. Locating the error in the code,
4. Correcting the incorrect code.

These steps are most beneficial when performed for each component (roughly each function) during the initial stages of programming, not by waiting until the entire program is written. It is common for a student to stare for hours at a program with an obscure error—it is hard to find the error when you are looking at the wrong code. By systematically testing each component in isolation, you isolate most errors and save a lot of time.

Let's look at the debugging steps in a little more detail:

Step 1: Determining that an error exists. This is generally the easiest step for programming assignments, and this is always the hardest step in large, "real world" programs. Just think about all the programs you have used that broke for some reason—these are clearly errors in the program that were not discovered when the program was written. In fact generally more hours are spent testing a program before it is sold than are spent writing it originally—and even then they missed some errors. However, most first-year programming courses make this step fairly easy by providing a project specification containing input and expected output. If your output doesn't match, then there is an error in the program. You might also have a more direct indicator that an error occurred if your program "crashes" (aborts abnormally), often with a cryptic error message. Congratulate yourself! You are done with the hardest step and you know that you have an error—now go identify it, find it and fix it.

Step 2: Identifying the type of error. There are many different ways to categorize errors, but for the purpose of debugging a program it is sufficient to answer two questions: Did the program produce some incorrect output, or did the execution go off track in some way (e.g., produce no output, run forever or generate an exception)? This classification does not tell you much about what the actual error is, but it does help you determine how to use print tracing to locate the bug. If some particular output value is incorrect, start your search by tracing changes to the variable that created the incorrect output; if, on the other hand, the execution followed some unexpected path, start tracing the execution flow from the earliest location at which you suspect that the execution went wild (or from the beginning of the program if you have no idea). Generally debugging involves print tracing of both data values and execution flow.

Step 3: Locating the error in the code. You already know where the bug occurred—somewhere between the beginning of the program and the site where you identified the bug. Now all you need to do is narrow the area to a single line in your program. How you go about doing that depends on the type of bug you have. If it is a bad value, locate each assignment to that variable in the code and add a print statement after the assignment to display the new value. When you identify the incorrect assignment, examine the expression on the right hand side of the assignment statement. The error is either in the expression or in one of the variables used in the expression. If it is an error in the expression, you have narrowed the error to a single expression—on to step 4. If it is a bad value in one of the variables in the expression, continue tracing variables. If you have determined that a variable's value is incorrect after it has been read in one of your input functions, then you have narrowed the problem down to a particular input operation.

If your program ends due to an uncaught exception, the error message will usually tell you exactly which line of your code was involved in causing the exception, and will print a stack trace showing which functions called your function and were called by it. Printing the values of the variables that occur on the line in your code referred to in the error message will often pinpoint the problem.

As mentioned earlier, sometimes programs fail without generating bad output values. They may perform some illegal operation (e.g., divide by zero) or terminate without producing any output. What is necessary in this case is to completely understand the path the program takes while executing. Fortunately, it can be fairly straightforward to follow even the most complex execution path by adding some well-placed print statements. Print statements at the beginning and end of each function will trace all function calls. Similarly, print statements at each control structure (`while` loop, `if` statement, `switch`, etc.) can trace the execution path within a function. Print tracing of the execution path is even more powerful when augmented with print tracing of data values. Perhaps the best example of this synergy is seen in printing all parameters at the entry to each function. Using the combination of execution path tracing and data tracing, it is possible to locate almost any error quickly, without getting stuck. If print tracing is applied to individual components during the initial coding of the program, errors can be quickly identified and corrected.

Step 4: Correcting the incorrect code. Once you have identified the location of the error, it may seem trivial to fix the code. This is often the case, but more often the error involves a misunderstanding about the operation of a function call to a large class library; fixing the error involves studying the interface specification documents for that class (and others that may be referred to by that function). Fortunately, there exists a wealth of information available to programmers, from numerous textbooks on the C++ language to web sites throughout the world containing detailed information on various libraries, complete with examples.

If the error still resists your efforts at correction, it is often useful to put down the program you are having difficulty with and work on a small test program related to the error until you really understand the operation of the class, function or piece of code you are using.

3.2.1 Example 1: School is more than studying

Let's look at some simple examples to illustrate the process of using print tracing to locate errors. At the same time, we will show some of the most common errors for new C++ programmers. The first program examines scores for a sporting event and prints out the winning team and score. The program loads scores for 4 events in women's gymnastics—vault, uneven bars, balance beam and floor exercise—then calculates the total score, determines the winning team, and prints the name of the winning team along with its score.

Note that some blank lines have been deliberately left in this code to leave room for adding print tracing statements later.

```
#include <iostream>
#include <fstream>
#include <string>
using namespace std;

int main ()
{
    double vault, floor, beam, bars, score, topscore;
    string school, winner;
        ifstream infile;
        infile.open("testfile.txt");
```

```
        if (!infile.good())
        {
            cerr << "Error: could not open testfile.txt" << endl;
            exit(-1);
        }

        topscore = 0;

        while (infile >> school)
        {

            infile >> vault;
            infile >> floor;
            infile >> beam;
            infile >> bars;



            score = vault + floor + beam + bars;

            if (score > topscore)
            {
               topscore = score;
               winner = school;
            }

    } // end while
    infile.close();

    cout << "The winner is " << winner
         << " with a score of " << topscore << endl;

    return 0;
    } // end main()
```

To run this example we use the scores from the 2005 NCAA Women's Gymnastics Championship. The text file contains lines with a team name followed by the team score for each of 4 apparatus. There is a **<tab>** character between the team name and scores and a tab between the scores for each apparatus. The test input file contains the following six lines:

Michigan	**49.050**	**49.225**	**48.900**	**49.400**
California - Los Angeles	**49.450**	**49.275**	**48.925**	**49.500**
Alabama	**49.625**	**49.325**	**48.850**	**49.600**
Georgia	**49.575**	**49.375**	**49.350**	**49.525**
Nebraska	**49.000**	**49.150**	**49.075**	**49.200**
Utah	**49.375**	**49.375**	**49.250**	**49.275**

When this program is executed it generates the following output:

The winner is Michigan with a score of 196.575

The output looks good, but is it correct? Unfortunately, it is very common for programmers to assume that since the output is reasonable, the program must be correct. After all, the code made sense when it was written, so it is probably correct. For this program it is easy to determine the correct scores for each team, and doing so shows that Georgia was the winner with a score of 197.825. What went wrong with the program?

To find the error, we need more information about the actual execution of the program, including changes to the variables. In the second version of this program, we do not intend to fix the error, only to add some statements to print the contents of certain variables in the `while` loop (lines **18-33**) to track the processing of the input file. In the following code, we show the debug statements in **bold**.

```
1: #include <iostream>
2: #include <fstream>
3: #include <string>
4: using namespace std;

5: #define DEBUG (true)

6: int main ()
7: {
8:     double vault, floor, beam, bars, score, topscore;
9:     string school, winner;
10:    ifstream infile;

11:    infile.open("testfile.txt");
12:    if (!infile.good())
13:    {
```

```
14:         cerr << "Error: could not open testfile.txt" << endl;
15:         exit(-1);
16:     }

17:     topscore = 0;

18:     while (infile >> school)
19:     {

20:         infile >> vault;
21:         infile >> floor;
22:         infile >> beam;
23:         infile >> bars;
24:

25:         if (DEBUG) cout <<school<< " " <<vault<< " " <<floor
26:                         << " " <<beam << " " << bars <<endl;

27:         score = vault + floor + beam + bars;

28:         if (score > topscore)
29:         {
30:             topscore = score;
31:             winner = school;
32:         }

33:     } // end while
34:     infile.close();

35:     cout << "The winner is " << winner
36:          << " with a score of " << topscore << endl;

37:     return 0;
38: } // end main()
```

The first thing to notice in this version of our program is a macro definition of **DEBUG** on line **5**. All later occurrences of **DEBUG** will be replaced with the `bool` value (**true**). This will be used to control whether print tracing is performed throughout the program and will enable us to leave the debug code in the program after we have completed the debug process. Next, we add a print statement in lines **25** and **26** to echo each input line read from the file. The print statement is also placed in an *if-statement* so that the debug definition can control whether printing occurs—remember that the value of **DEBUG** is (true).

Now when we re-execute the program, it will include additional output that, hopefully, will illuminate the error. The output for the second version of the program is:

Michigan 49.05 49.225 48.9 49.4
California 49.05 49.225 48.9 49.4
The winner is Michigan with a score of 196.575

The first two lines are debugging output and the third line is the same, incorrect program output as in the first version of the program. Clearly something is wrong with the processing in the loop. First, only two of the six teams had scores processed. In fact, the second team scores are incorrect, matching the Michigan scores even though the input file contains different values. But the scores are not the first error; that occurs in reading in the team name "California - Los Angeles". Only the first word is placed in the variable (`school`). What happen to the remainder of the name? It was not input, so it must still be in the input buffer. This means it will be read by the next input line (line **20**) which expects a numeric value for the vault score. Of course the character '-' is not a number, so the file input fails, preventing further input and leaving the current value in the variable (**`vault`**) unchanged. The fail state for the input file also prevents all subsequent loads from modifying variables and terminates the loop after the second iteration. At this point, we have identified the input to the variable school as the line of the code causing the error (**line 18**), but it may take some investigation of how file input is performed to determine the reason for the error. The ">>" input operator uses "whitespace" to partition strings read from the file. Whitespace includes tabs, spaces and newline characters. So when the school name is read, the space between "California" and "- Los Angeles" terminates the read. This does not match the requirements that all items in the input file are delimited by tab characters (not spaces).

We need to change the way the school name is read to allow spaces in the name. This can be done using the **`getline(ifstream, string, char)`** function that reads from an **`ifstream`**, into a **`string`** until a delimiting **`char`** is found. By specifying that the delimiting character is the tab character, `getline()` will place all characters up to the tab character in the `school` string. The third, and final, version of this program includes the correct function to read the school name allowing spaces in the name (line **18**).

```
1: #include <iostream>
2: #include <fstream>
3: #include <string>
4: using namespace std;
```

```
#define DEBUG (false)

int main ()
{
    double vault, floor, beam, bars, score, topscore;
    string school, winner;
    ifstream infile;

    infile.open("testfile.txt");
    if (!infile.good())
    {
        cerr << "Error: could not open testfile.txt" << endl;
        exit(-1);
    }

    topscore = 0;

    while (getline(infile, school, '\t'))
    {

        infile >> vault;
        infile >> floor;
        infile >> beam;
        infile >> bars;
        infile.ignore(100, '\n'); // consume rest of line

        if (DEBUG) cout <<school<< " " <<vault<< " " <<floor
                        << " " <<beam << " " << bars <<endl;

        score = vault + floor + beam + bars;

        if (score > topscore)
        {
            topscore = score;
            winner = school;
        }

    } // end while
    infile.close();
```

```
35:     cout << "The winner is " << winner
36:           << " with a score of " << topscore << endl;

37:     return 0;
38: } // end main()
```

Let's take a closer look at the final version of this program. We have modified two lines in addition to the fix on line **18**. Debug printing at lines **25** and **26** was retained, but the printing is now suppressed by changing the value of **DEBUG** to (**false**) in line **5**. Finally, we added a new function call `infile.ignore()` in line **24** to read the remaining characters in each line of input data. This is required because the `getline()` function (line **18**) does not eliminate any whitespace preceding the school name – as the use of the input (>>) operator does. For this input file, the `ignore` function reads the `newline` character so that it is not considered to be part of thė next school name. When we re-execute this version of the program we get the correct output:

The winner is Georgia with a score of 197.825

There is a lot to digest in this example. We showed how to use print statements to trace both execution flow (which iteration of the loop failed) and data flow (how "California - Los Angeles" was incorrectly read using the >> input operator). We showed how the use of a macro (**DEBUG**) along with `if` statements can control whether debug printing occurs. We applied this debugging technique to one of the most common programming errors: incorrectly reading/parsing some input data. As an exercise, think about how you might debug this program if the input data came directly from the 2005 NCAA Women's Gymnastics web page. How would the program find that page? How many network class definitions would you need to understand to get to that web page? How would you parse the text on that page to extract the scores? How many things could go wrong?

3.2.2 Example 2: Traveling to lose (or gain) weight!

The next example illustrates how a misunderstanding of a control statement can lead to incorrect output and, more importantly, how this type of bug can be systematically found and corrected. This program asks a person's weight and travel plans, then determines the person's new weight at their destination (another planet in our solar system). The input consists of a person's earth weight and the destination planet (we ignore a large number of physical properties that make the travel—or living—impractical). For simplicity, and to show another form of program input, the person's weight and planet number will be specified as command line arguments to the program. If you have not seen command line argument before, they are arguments to the main() function in the form of an integer count of the number of arguments (**`argc`**) and an array of pointers to the C-strings containing the arguments (**`*argv[]`**). For this program the value of `argc` should be 3 since there will be three arguments given when the program is executed; `arvg[0]` will contain the name of the program, `argv[1]` will hold the string representation of the travelers weight, and `argv[2]` will identify which planet the person has traveled to. The original (incorrect) example solution is:

```
#include <iostream>
#include <iomanip>
using namespace std;

double calculateWeight (double, int);

int main( int argc, char *argv[] )
{
    double newWeight;
    if (argc != 3)
    {
        cout <<"Usage: example2 <weight> <planet(0-9)>" << endl;
        exit(-1);
    }

    newWeight = calculateWeight(atof(argv[1]), atoi(argv[2]));
    cout << "Your new weight is: " << newWeight;
} // end main()

double calculateWeight ( double earthLBS, int planet )
{
    double newLBS;

        switch (planet)
        {
         case 1: newLBS = earthLBS * .08;

         case 2: newLBS = earthLBS * .89;

```

```
          case 3: newLBS = earthLBS * 1.0;
          case 4: newLBS = earthLBS * .38;
          case 5: newLBS = earthLBS * 2.8;
          case 6: newLBS = earthLBS * .98;
          case 7: newLBS = earthLBS * 1.2;
          case 8: newLBS = earthLBS * .78;
          case 9: newLBS = earthLBS * .07;
          default:newLBS = earthLBS * 0.0;
     } // end switch
     return newLBS;
} // end calculateWeight()
```

You might see the error right now—it is a very common mistake. However, whether you see the error or not, it is the process of debugging this type of error that you should be learning. When you run this program with a weight of 125 and the planet number 3 (you are staying on Earth), you should calculate a new weight of 125. Unfortunately, when this program is executed it prints:

Your new weight is: 0

This is a "bad output data" error, but what is the cause? Using the systematic approach to print tracing, we should print out each change to the variable being output, such as **newWeight** in the `main()` function. As we saw in the first example, it can also be useful to print out the input values to make sure we are not performing the new weight calculation on bad input values. The modified version of this program is:

```
#include <iostream>
#include <iomanip>
using namespace std;

#define DEBUG (true)

double calculateWeight (double, int);

int main( int argc, char *argv[] )
{
    double newWeight;
    if (argc != 3)
    {
        cout <<"Usage: example2 <weight> <planet(0-9)>" << endl;
        exit(-1);
    }
    if (DEBUG)
        cout << "weight: "<< argv[1]<< "; planet: "<< argv[2]
             <<endl;


    newWeight = calculateWeight(atof(argv[1]), atoi(argv[2]));
    cout << "Your new weight is: " << newWeight;
} // end main()

double calculateWeight ( double earthLBS, int planet )
{
    double newLBS;

    switch (planet)
    {
        case 1: newLBS = earthLBS * .08;


        case 2: newLBS = earthLBS * .89;


        case 3: newLBS = earthLBS * 1.0;

```

```
         case 4: newLBS = earthLBS * .38;
         case 5: newLBS = earthLBS * 2.8;
        case 6: newLBS = earthLBS * .98;
        case 7: newLBS = earthLBS * 1.2;
        case 8: newLBS = earthLBS * .78;
        case 9: newLBS = earthLBS * .07;
        default:newLBS = earthLBS * 0.0;
    } // end switch
    return newLBS;
} // end calculateWeight()
```

Executing this modified program outputs the following debug message:

weight: 125; planet: 3

So, we are correctly reading the arguments, but the result is still incorrect. Since `newWeight` is assigned the value returned by `calculateWeight()`, we must continue debugging in `calculateWeight()`. To do this, we will add print statements to display changes to the variable `newLBS` since it is used to return the function value. These changes are shown below:

```
#include <iostream>
#include <iomanip>
using namespace std;

#define DEBUG (true)
```

```
double calculateWeight (double, int);

int main( int argc, char *argv[] )
{
    double newWeight;
    if (argc != 3)
    {
        cout <<"Usage: example2 <weight> <planet(0-9)>" << endl;
        exit(-1);
    }
    if (DEBUG)
        cout << "weight: "<< argv[1]<< "; planet: "<< argv[2]
               <<endl;


    newWeight = calculateWeight(atof(argv[1]), atoi(argv[2]));
    cout << "Your new weight is: " << newWeight;
} // end main()

double calculateWeight ( double earthLBS, int planet )
{
    double newLBS;

    switch (planet)
    {
    case 1: newLBS = earthLBS * .08;
            if (DEBUG){cout << "Case1: newLBS: " << newLBS <<
            endl;}

    case 2: newLBS = earthLBS * .89;
            if (DEBUG){cout << "Case2: newLBS: " << newLBS <<
            endl;}

    case 3: newLBS = earthLBS * 1.0;
            if (DEBUG){cout << "Case3: newLBS: " << newLBS <<
            endl;}

    case 4: newLBS = earthLBS * .38;
            if (DEBUG){cout << "Case4: newLBS: " << newLBS <<
            endl;}
```

```
    case 5: newLBS = earthLBS * 2.8;
            if (DEBUG){cout << "Case5: newLBS: " << newLBS << endl;}
    case 6: newLBS = earthLBS * .98;
            if (DEBUG){cout << "Case6: newLBS: " << newLBS << endl;}
    case 7: newLBS = earthLBS * 1.2;
            if (DEBUG){cout << "Case7: newLBS: " << newLBS << endl;}
    case 8: newLBS = earthLBS * .78;
            if (DEBUG){cout << "Case8: newLBS: " << newLBS << endl;}
    case 9: newLBS = earthLBS * .07;
            if (DEBUG){cout << "Case9: newLBS: " << newLBS << endl;}
    default:newLBS = earthLBS * 0.0;
            if (DEBUG){cout << "Default: newLBS: " << newLBS << endl;}
    } // end switch
    return newLBS;
} // end calculateWeight()
```

When this version of the program is executed, the following text is printed:

EarthWeight: 125; planetNumber 3
EarthLBS: 125; planet: 3
Case 3: newLBS: 125
Case 4: newLBS: 47.125
Case 5: newLBS: 295.5
Case 6: newLBS: 114.5
Case 7: newLBS: 111.125
Case 8: newLBS: 140.625
Case 9: newLBS: 8.375
Default: newLBS: 0
NewWeight: 0

Our print tracing shows the error in execution flow in this program. The switch statement branched to the correct case, but continued execution through all subsequent cases including the default, which sets the **`newLBS`** variable to 0. To correct this code, `break` statements should be added to each case block. This is one of the most common errors for new programmers; so common that it is useful to include print trace code whenever using `switch` statements (at least for the default case). The correct, final version is shown below with the **DEBUG** variable set to false to suppress the print statements used in debugging.

```
#include <iostream>
#include <iomanip>
using namespace std;

#define DEBUG (false)

double calculateWeight (double, int);

int main( int argc, char *argv[] )
{
    double newWeight;
    if (argc != 3)
    {
        cout <<"Usage: example2 <weight> <planet(0-9)>" << endl;
        exit(-1);
    }
    if (DEBUG)
        cout << "weight: "<< argv[1]<< "; planet: "<< argv[2]
             <<endl;


    newWeight = calculateWeight(atof(argv[1]), atoi(argv[2]));
    cout << "Your new weight is: " << newWeight;
} // end main()

double calculateWeight ( double earthLBS, int planet )
{
    double newLBS;

    switch (planet)
    {
```

```
    case 1: newLBS = earthLBS * .08;
            if (DEBUG){cout << "Case1: newLBS: " << newLBS << endl;}
            break;
    case 2: newLBS = earthLBS * .89;
            if (DEBUG){cout << "Case2: newLBS: " << newLBS << endl;}
            break;
    case 3: newLBS = earthLBS * 1.0;
            if (DEBUG){cout << "Case3: newLBS: " << newLBS << endl;}
            break;
    case 4: newLBS = earthLBS * .38;
            if (DEBUG){cout << "Case4: newLBS: " << newLBS << endl;}
            break;
    case 5: newLBS = earthLBS * 2.8;
            if (DEBUG){cout << "Case5: newLBS: " << newLBS << endl;}
            break;
    case 6: newLBS = earthLBS * .98;
            if (DEBUG){cout << "Case6: newLBS: " << newLBS << endl;}
            break;
    case 7: newLBS = earthLBS * 1.2;
            if (DEBUG){cout << "Case7: newLBS: " << newLBS << endl;}
            break;
    case 8: newLBS = earthLBS * .78;
            if (DEBUG){cout << "Case8: newLBS: " << newLBS << endl;}
            break;
    case 9: newLBS = earthLBS * .07;
            if (DEBUG){cout << "Case9: newLBS: " << newLBS << endl;}
            break;
    default:newLBS = earthLBS * 0.0;
            if (DEBUG){cout << "Default: newLBS: " << newLBS << endl;}
```

```
    } // end switch
    return newLBS;
} // end calculateWeight()
```

When the final version of this program is executed with arguments 125 and 3 the following, correct output is written:

Your new weight is: 125

3.2.3 Example 3: Stock Trading

The final example in this section illustrates some of the difficulties in using print tracing without careful thought. The program automates trading decisions for a simplified stock trading environment. The goal of the program is to find good trading heuristics for stock trading. For the purposes of this example, we have greatly simplified the trading patterns by simply using a random number generator to determine whether the stock traded up or down each day ^ so it will be impossible to find a heuristic that trades better than random. However, as an example, we will use a simple trading strategy that calculates an expected value and compares that to the current value to see whether we should buy (or sell) a single share of stock. Trading ends when the program has either doubled the original $1000 cash or halved it ($500). Here is the first attempt at the trading program.

```
#include <iostream>
#include <iomanip>
#include <string>
#include <stdlib.h> // need for rand()
#include <time.h>//need for rand()

using namespace std;

    double cash = 1000.00, stockPrice = 10.0, expectedPrice;
    int stockShares;

int main( )
{
    srand(time(NULL));
```

```
cout << fixed << showpoint << setprecision(2);
bool keepTrading = true;

while (keepTrading)
{
    stockPrice=stockPrice+(double)(rand()-RAND_MAX/2)/RAND_MAX;
    if (stockPrice <=0) stockPrice = 0.02;

    expectedPrice=stockPrice+(double)(rand()-RAND_MAX/2)/RAND_MAX;

    if (cash > stockPrice && expectedPrice > stockPrice*1.01)
    {
        cash = cash - stockPrice;
        stockShares = stockShares + 1;
    }

    if (stockShares > 0 && expectedPrice*1.02 < stockPrice)
    {
        cash = cash + stockPrice;
        stockShares = stockShares - 1;
    }

    if (cash+stockShares*stockPrice == 500) keepTrading = false;
    if (cash+stockShares*stockPrice == 2000) keepTrading = false;
} // end while
cout << "You now have $" << (cash+stockShares*stockPrice)
     << endl;
} // end main()
```

If you run this program, you might think that it would print out a cash value of under \$500 or over \$2000 (certainly nothing in between). It is theoretically possible that the program will not complete in any given amount of time if you continually trade in the range of \$500 to \$2000; however, this is extraordinarily unlikely over more than a second or two since that is sufficient time to make millions of trades. However if you run this program in its current form, it is almost certain that it will not complete in a second or two (or in the time it takes to read this book). While it is running, let us consider how to debug the program using the debugging approach in this section.

Step 1: Determine that an error exists. Well, the program has not terminated in "a reasonable amount of time", so it is likely that there is an error. The statistical nature of this particular program makes it impossible to prove that there is an error; however, time is better spent assuming that there is an error and trying to identify it than waiting for the program to complete, assuming no error exists and the program is just running an extraordinarily long time.

Step 2: Identifying the type of error. The program has not produced incorrect output—in fact it has not produced any output or even completed execution. So, we should first start by understanding the execution flow of the program.

Step 3: Locating the error in the code. We can use print tracing for this purpose, but there are some danger signs—the most important of which is that the program has been running for several minutes and it is possible to execute billions, or even trillions, of print statements in that time period. Inserting a bunch of print statements and re-executing the program is likely to generate an infinite stream of output—hopefully to your screen and not redirected to a printer! There are a couple of ways to deal with this problem: we can limit the frequency of printing, or we can add a new termination condition that is guaranteed to end the program much sooner than it is currently ending.

In this particular program, the primary execution path is through the loop starting at line **18** and continuing to line **41**. We could put a print statement at the beginning of the loop, but we expect it to iterate millions of times each second. It is more useful to iterate for only the first 5 times to see if the stock value, trading and cash values are correctly computed. This will reduce the information sent to the screen. We can clean up the debug output further by writing a new function that prints all the information helpful to debugging this program, including program variables and some expressions (like the total value of stock and cash). The following code shows our first attempt at print tracing this program.

```
1: #include <iostream>
2: #include <iomanip>
3: #include <string>
4: #include <stdlib.h> // need for rand()
5: #include <time.h>//need for rand()
6:
```

```
using namespace std;

double cash = 1000.00, stockPrice = 10.0, expectedPrice;
int stockShares;

void DEBUG_print(string,int); // debugging function
#define DEBUG (true)
int DEBUG_counter=0;

int main( )
{

    srand(time(NULL));
    cout << fixed << showpoint << setprecision(2);
    bool keepTrading = true;

    while (keepTrading)
    {
        if (DEBUG) DEBUG_print("",DEBUG_counter++);

        stockPrice = stockPrice+(double)(rand()-RAND_MAX/2)/
        RAND_MAX;
        if (stockPrice <=0) stockPrice = 0.02;

        expectedPrice = stockPrice+(double)(rand()-RAND_MAX/2)/
        RAND_MAX;

        if (cash > stockPrice && expectedPrice > stockPrice*1.01)
        {
            cash = cash - stockPrice;
            stockShares = stockShares + 1;
            if (DEBUG) DEBUG_print("buy",stockShares);
        }

        if (stockShares > 0 && expectedPrice*1.02 < stockPrice)
        {
            if (DEBUG) DEBUG_print("sell",stockShares);
```

```
35:             cash = cash + stockPrice;
36:             stockShares = stockShares - 1;
37:     }

38:         if (cash+stockShares*stockPrice == 500) keepTrading =
            false;
39:         if (cash+stockShares*stockPrice == 2000) keepTrading =
            false;
40:         if (DEBUG && DEBUG_counter == 5) keepTrading = false;
41:     } // end while
42:     cout << "You now have $" << (cash+stockShares*stockPrice)
            << endl;
43: } // end main()

44: void DEBUG_print(string msg, int num )
45: {
46:
47:         cout << "[" << msg << num << "]"
48:              << ": cash = " << cash
49:              << ": stockShares = " << stockShares
50:              << ": stockPrice = " << stockPrice
51:              << ": value = " << (cash+stockShares*stockPrice)
                 << endl;

52: } // end DEBUG_print()
```

As in the previous examples, we define the macro **DEBUG** to control the printing of debugging output (line **11**). In addition, we declare a debug variable to enable early termination of the program (**`DEBUG_counter`**). This variable is initialized to 0 (line **12**) and incremented each loop iteration (line **22**) and used to terminate the loop after 5 iterations (line **40**). This will ensure that the loop, and therefore the program, terminates - remember, at this time, we are only trying to determine if the algorithm is updating the variables correctly. We also choose to add print statements at three locations in the loop: at the start of each iteration (line **22**), after a share of stock is purchased (line **30**), and when a share of stock is sold (line **34**). At each of these locations it is useful to print out a variety of data values as well as the total stock plus cash value used to terminate the program. As in any program, instead of duplicating code throughout the program, it is better coding style to write a function that can be called from each site. We declare the new function **DEBUG_print** at lines **44** to **52**. This function prints the values of the variables **`cash`**, **`stockShares`** and **`stockPrice`** as well as the expression (**`cash + stockShares x stockPrice`**). It also prints a `string` argument that is used to identify the location of the call to **DEBUG_print** and can provide additional information relevant to that location. The first call to **DEBUG_print** (line **22**) passes a null string along with the loop iteration counter stored in the variable **DEBUG_counter**. The second call to **DEBUG_print** (at line **30**) passes the string "**buy**" to indicate that this debug output was generated when a share of stock was purchased, as well as the numer of shares currently owned (**stockShares**). Similarly, the third call to **DEBUG_print** (at line **34**) passes the string "**sell**" to indicate that the program is selling a share of stock, along with the shares owned. When the modified program is executed, the following output is produced (note that due to the random nature of the calculation of **stockPrice** and **expectedPrice**, different output is likely for each run):

```
1:     cash=1000.00: stockShares=0: stockPrice=10.00: value=1000.00
2:     cash=1000.00: stockShares=0: stockPrice=10.23: value=1000.00
buy1:  cash=988.20:  stockShares=1: stockPrice=11.80: value=1000.00
3:     cash=988.20:  stockShares=1: stockPrice=10.30: value=998.50
4:     cash=988.20:  stockShares=1: stockPrice=12.50: value= 1000.70
buy2:  cash=976.10:  stockShares=2: stockPrice=12.10: value=1000.30
5:     cash=976.10:  stockShares=2: stockPrice=10.50: value=997.10
sell2: cash=989.10:  stockShares=2: stockPrice=13.00: value=1002.10
```

This output shows 5 cycles of trading with two shares purchased and one share sold. It appears that buying and selling stock operate correctly and that the calculation of the total value is correct. We have not yet identified the error, but we have tested a significant portion of the program. Unfortunately, the error doesn't manifest during the first few iterations of the loop, so we need to continue execution beyond 5 iterations. This can be easily achieved by changing the constant 5 in line **40** to a much larger value (say 5000), but this will generate a large number of output lines that must be examined. We will use a new technique to reduce the total debug output generated: limit the frequency of printing by only printing out debugging values every 1000 iterations. This can be achieved in a number of ways, the easiest of which is to add a single line to **DEBUG_print()** to only print if **DEBUG_counter** is a multiple of 1000. This is shown below:

```
1: #include <iostream>
2: #include <iomanip>
3: #include <string>
4: #include <stdlib.h> // need for rand()
5: #include <time.h> // need for rand()
6:
7: using namespace std;

8: double cash = 1000.00, stockPrice = 10.0, expectedPrice;
9: int stockShares;
```

```
void DEBUG_print(string,int); // debugging function
#define DEBUG (true)
int DEBUG_counter=0;

int main( )
{

   srand(time(NULL));
   cout << fixed << showpoint << setprecision(2);
   bool keepTrading = true;

   while (keepTrading)
   {
      if (DEBUG) DEBUG_print("",DEBUG_counter++);

      stockPrice = stockPrice+(double)(rand()-RAND_MAX/2)/
      RAND_MAX;
      if (stockPrice <=0) stockPrice = 0.02;

      expectedPrice = stockPrice+(double)(rand()-RAND_MAX/2)/
      RAND_MAX;

      if (cash > stockPrice && expectedPrice > stockPrice*1.01)
      {
          cash = cash - stockPrice;
          stockShares = stockShares + 1;
      if (DEBUG) DEBUG_print("buy",stockShares);
                      }

      if (stockShares > 0 && expectedPrice*1.02 < stockPrice)
      {
      if (DEBUG) DEBUG_print(“sell”,stockShares);
          cash = cash + stockPrice;
          stockShares = stockShares - 1;
      }
```

```
38:         if (cash+stockShares*stockPrice == 500) keepTrading =
            false;
39:         if (cash+stockShares*stockPrice == 2000) keepTrading =
            false;
40:         if (DEBUG && DEBUG_counter == 5000) keepTrading =
            false;
41: } // end while
42: cout << "You now have $" << (cash+stockShares*stockPrice)
            << endl;
43: } // end main()

44: void DEBUG_print(string msg, int num )
45: {
46:         if (DEBUG_counter % 1000 == 0)
47:         cout << "[" << msg << num << "]"
48:              << ": cash = " << cash
49:              << ": stockShares = " << stockShares
50:              << ": stockPrice = " << stockPrice
51:              << ": value = " << (cash+stockShares*stockPrice)
                 << endl;

52: } // end DEBUG_print()
```

The first change made in this version of the program modifies the expression at line **40**, changing 5 to 5000 to enable more iterations of the loop before program termination. The second change inserts an if statement at line **46** that restricts the printing of debug information to only those iterations that are multiples of 1000 (i.e. at iterations 1000, 2000, 3000, etc.). When this version of the program is executed the following output is generated:

```
1000: cash=804.00:    stockShares=11: stockPrice=6.02:  value=870.22
2000: cash=436.20:    stockShares=35: stockPrice=12.23: value=864.25
3000: cash=500.82:    stockShares=68: stockPrice=24.31: value=2153.90
4000: cash=1150.13:   stockShares=33: stockPrice=8.50:  value=1430.63
sell32: cash=1159.23: stockShares=32: stockPrice= 9.10: value=1450.43
5000: cash=820.10:    stockShares=40: stockPrice=15.50: value=1440.01
```

When we re-execute, printing every 1000th iteration, it becomes apparent that the error involves the exit condition of the loop because the total value exceeded the $2000 limit at iteration 3000 (**value = 2153.90**). This isolates the error to line **39**.

Step 4: Correcting the incorrect code. At this point the error is easy to detect and simple to fix. The expression in line **39**:

```
(cash + stockShares*stockPrice == 2000)
```

fails to account for the extremely likely case that the value may exceed $2000 instead of being exactly $2000. To fix the error, simply change the **equal to** operator (==) to the **greater than or equal to** operator (>=). Go ahead and make that change, but stop and think about how this will affect the program as a whole. You should also change the expression on line **38** to make sure you terminate the program if the value drops below $500. What would happen if you only changed the expression in line **39**? How would you debug that program, and which step would be the most difficult to complete?

Here is the final version of this program with the expressions on lines **38** and **39** corrected and the macro **DEBUG** set to false (on line 11) to suppress debugging output:

```
1: #include <iostream>
2: #include <iomanip>
3: #include <string>
4: #include <stdlib.h> // need for rand()
5: #include <time.h> // need for rand()
6:
7: using namespace std;

8: double cash = 1000.00, stockPrice = 10.0, expectedPrice;
9: int stockShares;

10: void DEBUG_print(string,int); // debugging function
11: #define DEBUG (false)
12: int DEBUG_counter=0;

13: int main( )
14: {

15:     srand(time(NULL));
16:     cout << fixed << showpoint << setprecision(2);
17:     bool keepTrading = true;

18:     while (keepTrading)
```

```
    {


        if (DEBUG) DEBUG_print("",DEBUG_counter++);

        stockPrice = stockPrice+(double)(rand()-RAND_MAX/2)/
        RAND_MAX;
        if (stockPrice <=0) stockPrice = 0.02;

        expectedPrice = stockPrice+(double)(rand()-RAND_MAX/2)/
        RAND_MAX;

        if (cash > stockPrice && expectedPrice > stockPrice*1.01)
        {
            cash = cash - stockPrice;
            stockShares = stockShares + 1;
            if (DEBUG) DEBUG_print("buy",stockShares);
        }

        if (stockShares > 0 && expectedPrice*1.02 < stockPrice)
        {
            if (DEBUG) DEBUG_print(“sell”,stockShares);
            cash = cash + stockPrice;
            stockShares = stockShares - 1;
        }

        if (cash+stockShares*stockPrice <= 500) keepTrading =
        false;
        if (cash+stockShares*stockPrice >= 2000) keepTrading =
        false;
        if (DEBUG && DEBUG_counter == 5000) keepTrading =
        false;
} // end while
cout << "You now have $" << (cash+stockShares*stockPrice)
<< endl;
} // end main()

void DEBUG_print(string msg, int num )
{
```

```
if (DEBUG_counter % 1000 == 0)
        cout << "[" << msg << num << "]"
        << ": cash = " << cash
        << ": stockShares = " << stockShares
        << ": stockPrice = " << stockPrice
        << ": value = " << (cash+stockShares*stockPrice)
        << endl;

} // end DEBUG_print()
```

When this final version of the program is executed, it will terminate when the value of stock and cash either exceeds $2000 or falls below $500 and prints the amount. For instance, when we ran the corrected program it completed with the following output:

You now have $489.78

3.3 USING EXCEPTIONS AND ASSERTIONS TO AID IN FINDING OR AVOIDING ERRORS

While the purpose of the chapter has been to show how print statements can be used to identify and correct errors in an existing program, it is often more efficient to place some debugging information in the code as it is being created. In this section, we will examine two proactive measures to reduce common program errors: exception handling of parameters and assertions.

3.3.1 Exception Handling for Parameter Checking

The C++ language includes an extensive exception handling mechanism to improve program management of error conditions. If you have written even relatively small C++ programs, you are probably familiar with some exceptions. One of the more powerful management capabilities is the verification of parameter value ranges for function calls. If we can identify invalid parameters when a function is called, the error is less likely to manifest inside the function and therefore easier to trace to the bad function call. This is best illustrated by revisiting the `calculateWeight()` function in example 2. What would happen if the function was called with the planet argument asking for the weight on the 10th planet? Or the 15th planet? These values are invalid since it is meaningless to indicate planets that do not exist. It is better to identify the error directly (as an invalid argument to `calculateWeight()`) than to simply report a default weight of 0. The `IllegalArgumentException` class is designed to manage this event. In the following code, we add parameter checking to `calculateWeight()`:

```
#include <iostream>
#include <iomanip>
```

```
#include <stdexcept>

using namespace std;

#define DEBUG (false)

double calculateWeight (double, int);

int main( int argc, char *argv[] )
{
 double newWeight;
 if (argc != 3)
 {
   cout <<"Usage: example2 <weight> <planet(0-9)>" << endl;
   exit(-1);
 }
 if (DEBUG)
   cout << "weight: "<< argv[1]<< "; planet: "<< argv[2] <<endl;


 newWeight = calculateWeight(atof(argv[1]), atoi(argv[2]));
 cout << "Your new weight is: " << newWeight;
} // end main()

double calculateWeight ( double earthLBS, int planet )
{
 double newLBS;

if (planet < 0 || planet > 9) throw invalid_argument("unknown
 planet");

 switch (planet)
 {
   case 1: newLBS = earthLBS * .08;
           if (DEBUG){cout << "Case1: newLBS: " << newLBS
           << endl;}
           break;
   case 2: newLBS = earthLBS * .89;
```

```
            if (DEBUG){cout << "Case2: newLBS: " << newLBS << endl;}
            break;
    case 3: newLBS = earthLBS * 1.0;
            if (DEBUG){cout << "Case3: newLBS: " << newLBS << endl;}
            break;
    case 4: newLBS = earthLBS * .38;
            if (DEBUG){cout << "Case4: newLBS: " << newLBS << endl;}
            break;
    case 5: newLBS = earthLBS * 2.8;
            if (DEBUG){cout << "Case5: newLBS: " << newLBS << endl;}
            break;
    case 6: newLBS = earthLBS * .98;
            if (DEBUG){cout << "Case6: newLBS: " << newLBS << endl;}
            break;
    case 7: newLBS = earthLBS * 1.2;
            if (DEBUG){cout << "Case7: newLBS: " << newLBS << endl;}
            break;
    case 8: newLBS = earthLBS * .78;
            if (DEBUG){cout << "Case8: newLBS: " << newLBS << endl;}
            break;
    case 9: newLBS = earthLBS * .07;
            if (DEBUG){cout << "Case9: newLBS: " << newLBS << endl;}
            break;
    default:newLBS = earthLBS * 0.0;
            if (DEBUG){cout << "Default: newLBS: " << newLBS << endl;}

 } // end switch
 return newLBS;
} // end calculateWeight()
```

Now, if the function, `calculateWeight()`, is called with a planet outside the range of 1-9, an `invalid_argument` exception will be "thrown", terminating the function call. Any calling function can choose to "catch" the exception or, if uncaught, it will terminate the program. This takes the error handling code out of the function (which doesn't know how to fix anything). This is much easier to debug than if the program ran without an error being detected and returned my weight as 0. Is there any other parameter checking that should be performed? For very large programs, parameter checking is essential—without it an error may manifest anywhere in the program. In the unlikely event that we discover a new planet, this exception will identify the need to change the function. Again, the exception will make it easier to track the error (or outdated code) than returning the default weight of 0. This mechanism isn't foolproof—if astronomers decide that Pluto is not worthy of being labeled a planet (a question that arises occasionally) then the exception condition will fail to identify the change in specification (namely that there are now only 8 planets). Still using exceptions to verify parameter bounds is one of the most important preventative measures a programmer can take when writing code. It localizes the detection of errors, greatly simplifying the location of the erroneous code.

3.3.2 Assertion Checking

The C++ library also has an extension for placing assertions into program code. Assertions provide a powerful mechanism for testing assumptions made in the program without degrading program execution time. **`assert`** is a macro that aborts the program when the expression evaluates to false. To show how assertions can be added to the code, we will extend the stock trading example (`StockTrading`) to include the checks to make sure we do not iterate the loop when the total value of assets either exceeds $2000 or falls below $500. If either assertion fails, then the program must be incorrect since these are the two exit conditions of the loop.

```
#include <iostream>
#include <iomanip>
#include <string>
#include <stdlib.h> // need for rand()
#include <tie.h> // need for rand()

using namespace std;

 double cash = 1000.00, stockPrice = 10.0, expectedPrice;
 int stockShares;

void DEBUG_print(string,int); // debugging function
#define DEBUG (false)
int DEBUG_counter=0;
```

```
int main( )
{

   srand(time(NULL));
   cout << fixed << showpoint << setprecision(2);
   bool keepTrading = true;

   while (keepTrading)
   {

      assert(cash+stockShares*stockPrice < 2000);
      assert(cash+stockShares*stockPrice > 500);

      if (DEBUG) DEBUG_print("",DEBUG_counter++);

      stockPrice = stockPrice+(double)(rand()-RAND_MAX/2)/
      RAND_MAX;
      if (stockPrice <=0) stockPrice = 0.02;

      expectedPrice = stockPrice+(double)(rand()-RAND_MAX/2)/
      RAND_MAX;

       if (cash > stockPrice && expectedPrice > stockPrice*1.01)
       {
          cash = cash - stockPrice;
          stockShares = stockShares + 1;
          if (DEBUG) DEBUG_print(“buy”,stockShares);
       }

       if (stockShares > 0 && expectedPrice*1.02 < stockPrice)
       {
          if (DEBUG) DEBUG_print("sell",stockShares);
          cash = cash + stockPrice;
          stockShares = stockShares - 1;
       }
```

```
38:         if (cash+stockShares*stockPrice <= 500) keepTrading = false;
39:         if (cash+stockShares*stockPrice >= 2000) keepTrading = false;
40:         if (DEBUG && DEBUG_counter == 5000) keepTrading = false;
41:   } // end while
42:   cout << "You now have $" << (cash+stockShares*stockPrice) << endl;
43: } // end main()

44: void DEBUG_print(string msg, int num )
45: {
46:         if (DEBUG_counter % 1000 == 0)
47:         cout << "[" << msg << num << "]"
48:         << ": cash = " << cash
49:         << ": stockShares = " << stockShares
50:         << ": stockPrice = " << stockPrice
51:         << ": value = " << (cash+stockShares*stockPrice) << endl;

52: } // end DEBUG_print()
```

We added two assertions to this code at lines **20** and **21**. They calculate the total value of assets and check to see if the value is in the bounds $500 to $2000. If either of these assertions fail, the abort() function is called that on most compilers prints the file name and line number of the assertion failure.

CHAPTER 4

Trace Debugging for More Advanced C++ Constructs

4.1 CHAPTER OBJECTIVES

- To learn how to debug more advanced C++ constructs such as strings, pointers, and structs
- To apply the debugging techniques to object-oriented programming using classes

4.2 STRINGS

String variables are declared in the same manner as other variables like `int`, `float`, `double`, and `bool`. However, strings serve many more purposes than do numeric data and use a number of built-in C++ functions for assignment, concatenation, finding the string length, finding a substring, and comparing strings, to name a few.

Debugging traces can be inserted to display critical string variables before and after each use of a string function, which we summarize in Appendix B.2. This is illustrated in detail in Fig. 4.1, which shows the C++ source code to illustrate all the string functions mentioned previously. Trace statements are shown in boldface so we know the values of each string variable before and after its use in a string manipulation operation. A function called `testparam` is defined to illustrate the testing of string variables as both call-by-value and call-by-reference function parameters. Another function called `alpha_to_integer` (roughly equivalent to the C++ function `atoi`) is defined to illustrate the conversion of a string data type—consisting of some number of positive digits—into an integer data type.

We display the initial values of five string variables, `word1` through `word5`, using the `cout` statements in lines 23-27. The output of these values is shown in lines 2-6 of the output, shown after the code (Fig. 4.1).

```
/*Debugging Example - This program illustrates possible debugging
code insertions that would be useful for testing string
manipulation statements and string function calls. The program
output is shown below the program listing.*/

#include <iostream>
#include <string>
using namespace std;

//function prototypes
void testparam(string, string, string&);
int alpha_to_integer (string);

int main()
{
    string word1 = "Hail";
    string word2 = "my";
    string word3 = "Chief!";
    string word4;
    string word5 = "456";
    string nextsymbol1;
    string nextsymbol2;
    string nextsymbol3;
    int result = 0;

    cout << "BEGINNING OF TEST STRING PROGRAM OUTPUT." << endl;
    cout << "word1 (string) is: " << word1 << endl;
    cout << "word2 (string) is: " << word2 << endl;
    cout << "word3 (string) is: " << word3 << endl;
    cout << "word4 (string) is: " << word4 << endl;
    cout << "word5 (string) is: " << word5 << endl << endl;

    word4 = word1 + " to the " + word3;

    cout << "word4 concatenates word1 & word3 with \" to the \"
          in between: " << word4 << endl;
```

Figure 4.1

Example program and output for testing string functions

```
    if (word1 < word3)
          cout << "word1 is less than word3." << endl;
    else
          cout << "word1 is not less than word3." << endl;

    word4 = word3;

    cout << "Value of word4 (set to word3) is now: " << word4
         << endl << endl;

    testparam(word1, word2, word3);

cout << "Return from function testparam: word1, word2, word3: "
     << word1 << " " << word2 << " " << word3 << endl << endl;

    nextsymbol1 = word1.substr(0,1);
    nextsymbol2 = word1.substr(1,1);
    nextsymbol3 = word1.substr(2,1);

    cout << "Result of substring scan for first 3
         << individual symbols of word1 is: "
         << nextsymbol1 << " " << nextsymbol2 << " "
         << nextsymbol3 << endl;
    cout << "word3 string length is: " << word3.length() << endl;
    cout << "The substring of word3, index 3, length 2: "
         << word3.substr(3,2) << endl;

    word3 = word3 + word3;

    cout << "The concatenation of word3 to itself is: "
         << word3 << endl;
    cout << "word3 string length is now: " << word3.length()
         << endl << endl;

    result = alpha_to_integer(word5);

```

Figure 4.1 (Continued)

```
    cout \< "Result of converting string word5 to an integer is: "
         << result << endl << endl;
    cout << "END OF TEST STRING PROGRAM OUTPUT." << endl;

    return 0;
}

void testparam(string wordx, string wordy, string& wordz)
{
    cout << "Entering the function testparam." << endl;

    wordz = wordx + wordz;
}

int alpha_to_integer (string wordx)
{
    int i;
    int stringLength = wordx.length();
    int number = 0;
    char ch;

    cout << "Entering the alpha_to_integer function." << endl;

    for (i=0; i < stringLength; i++)
    {
         ch = wordx[i] - '0';
         number = number + ch*pow(10.0, stringLength - i -1);

         cout << "number is currently: " << number << endl;
    }
    return number;
}                    //end of example program code
```

```
BEGINNING OF TEST STRING PROGRAM OUTPUT.
word1 (string) is: Hail
word2 (string) is: my
word3 (string) is: Chief!
```

Figure 4.1 (Continued)

```
5  word4 (string) is:
6  word5 (string) is: 456
7
8  word4 concatenates word1 & word3 with " to the " in
9  between: Hail to the Chief!
10 word1 is not less than word3.
11 Value of word4 (set to word3) is now: Chief!
12
13 Entering the function testparam.
14 Return from function testparam: word1, word2, word3:
15 Hail my HailChief!
16
17 Result of substring scan for first 3 individual symbols of
   word1 is: H a i
18 word3 string length is: 10
19 The substring of word3, index 3, length 2 is: lC
20 The concatenation of word3 to itself is: HailChief!HailChief!
21 word3 string length is now: 20
22
23 Entering the alpha_to_integer function.
24 number is currently: 400
25 number is currently: 450
26 number is currently: 456
27 Result of converting string word5 to integer is: 456
28
29 END OF TEST STRING PROGRAM OUTPUT.
```

Figure 4.1 (Continued)

Concatenation is illustrated in line 29. The trace statement in line 31 produces the output in line 8, which verifies that the word "to the" is successfully inserted between `word1` and `word3`.

String comparison is made in line 32 and the output is shown in line 10, verifying that the first letter of `word1`, "H", is not less than the first letter of `word3`, "C". Simple string assignment is shown in line 37 where `word4` is set to the current value of `word3`, "Chief!". The output of this test is shown in line 11.

Strings as parameters to a function are tested in the function call of line 41 and the function `testparam` in lines 66-71. We see that `word1` is renamed `wordx` in the function, and `word2` is renamed `wordy`. `Word3` is renamed `wordz` in the function, and is also defined as a call-by-reference parameter to allow it to be changed by the function. The function then defines `wordz` (`word3` in `main`) as the concatenation of `wordx` (`word1` in `main`) and `wordz` (`word3` in `main`). When the function is entered during execution, that fact is displayed in line 13 using the code in line 68. After the function returns to main, the result of the function (the previous values for `word1` and `word2` and the new value for `word3`) is displayed in the output line 14 using the `cout` statement in line 43 in main.

The substring and length functions are illustrated in lines 45-56 in Fig. 4.1, with the output shown in lines 17-21. When `word3` is concatenated with itself, its length is doubled from 10 to 20.

The last segment of code in Fig. 4.1 is the function call (line 58) to `alpha_to_integer` to convert the string `word5` (value "456") to the integer 456. Trace statements in the function are shown in lines 80 and 87. Line 23 of the string test program output shows the output for the function entry statement. The output for the evolution of values for the variable `number` is shown in output lines 24-26, and the return value for `number` is shown in output line 27.

Note in line 78 that the character variable `ch` must be specified as a `char` and not a `string`; otherwise line 85 would generate a syntax error because a string variable `ch` would not be convertible to `double` to complete the multiplication with the double function `pow`. Note that no casting of `stringLength` is required in line 85 because C++ automatically converts integers to double before executing `pow`.

4.3 POINTERS

A pointer is an address of some variable or constant in C++. If the content of the pointer is `NULL`, then the pointer points to nothing (i.e. it contains no address). You can assign pointers to other pointers and use pointers in arithmetic expressions. Remember also that array names are actually treated as pointers, so that array names used as function parameters are actually pointers.

A pointer (called `mypointer`) to an integer variable (called `myvariable`) initialized to 100, is declared as:

```
int myvariable = 100;
int* mypointer = &myvariable; //or use int *mypointer = &myvariable;
```

The asterisk symbol (*) is used to designate a pointer. The ampersand symbol (&) is called *the address operator* and the expression `&myvariable` means "the address of `myvariable`". When the asterisk symbol is used next to a pointer in an expression, it is called the *dereferencing operator* and means "take the pointer value, an address, and find the value of the variable at that address". For instance,

```
int x = 0;
x = *mypointer -15;
cout << "The value of x is now: " << x << endl;
```

will display the value *85* for the variable *x*.

However, dropping the dereferencing operator from the second statement will result in a syntax error.

If we replace the second statement with

```
x = mypointer - 15;
```

we will get a syntax error `cannot convert int* to int`. Addresses should only be stored in declared pointers, and normal integer (or floating point, etc.) values should be stored in declared integer (or declared floating point, etc.) variables.

Programs with pointers can be debugged in a straightforward manner using the tracing techniques of Chapter 3 to record the values of pointers and other variables before and after they are read or updated by the program. In Fig. 4.2 a simple swap program is presented to illustrate the use of pointers. Tracing statements are shown in boldface type to help visualize how the pointer variables are changing. Lines 7 and 8 show the initial values of two variables, `mydata` and `yourdata`. In line 14 the `main` function calls the `swap` function with the addresses of `mydata` and `yourdata` as the calling parameters. The main code in the `swap` function is shown in lines 30-32. Here the integer variable `temp` is set to the current value of the pointer variable by the `mine` pointer, which is the variable in `main` called `mydata`. Its current value is 999. Then the code on line 31 in the `swap` function:

```
*mine = *yours;
```

is equivalent to the `main` function assignment:

```
mydata = yourdata;
```

Finally, the code on line 32,

```
*yours = temp;
```

puts the temp value 999 into the variable pointed to by `yours`, that is, `yourdata`.

```
/*Debugging Example - This program swaps the values of two integers in
main. It uses pointers as parameters in the swap function to access
the original data in main. */

1 #include <iostream>
2 using namespace std;
3 void swap (int*, int* );     //swap function prototype
4
```

Figure 4.2

Example program and output for testing pointers

```
int main()
{
    int mydata = 999;
    int yourdata = 1221;

    cout << "START OF MAIN (OUTPUT)." << endl;
    cout << "mydata (address) = " << &mydata << " yourdata (address) = "
         << &yourdata << endl;
    cout << "mydata = " <<mydata << " yourdata = " << yourdata
         << endl;                                   //prints 999 & 1221

    swap (&mydata, &yourdata); //calls swap with addresses of int
    variables

    cout << "mydata = " <<mydata << " yourdata = " << yourdata
         << endl;                                   //prints 1221 & 999
    cout << "END OF MAIN (OUTPUT)." << endl;

    return 0;
}

void swap (int* mine, int* yours)  //declares pointers to integers
{
    int temp = 0;

    cout << endl << "Entering swap function." << endl;
    cout << "mine (value) = " << mine << " yours (value) = "
         << yours << endl;
    cout << "Before the swap: temp = " << temp << " *mine (value) = "
         << *mine << " *yours (value) = " << *yours << endl;

    temp = *mine;          //mine points to "mydata" in main
                           //(value of 999), stores 999 in temp
    *mine = *yours;        //yours points to "yourdata" in main
                           //(value of 1221), stores 1221 in "mydata"
    *yours = temp;         //value of 999 in temp stored in "yourdata"
                           //in main, swap is complete
```

Figure 4.2 (Continued)

```
33
34     cout << "After the swap: temp = " << temp << " *mine (value) = "
           << *mine << " *yours (value) = " << *yours << endl;
35     cout << "Exiting swap function." << endl << endl;
36 }
```

```
START OF MAIN (OUTPUT).
mydata (address) = 0x073f7a3c yourdata (address) = 0x073f7a38
mydata = 999 yourdata = 1221

Entering swap function.
mine (value) = 0x073f7a3c yours (value) = 0x073f7a38
Before the swap: temp = 0 *mine (value) = 999 *yours (value) =
1221
After the swap: temp = 999 *mine (value) = 1221 *yours (value) =
999
Exiting swap function.

mydata = 1221 yourdata = 999
END OF MAIN (OUTPUT).
```

Figure 4.2 (Continued)

The tracing code displays the start and end of program execution in main (lines 10 and 17), the entering and exiting of the swap function (lines 26 and 35), and the pointer values of `mine` (which has the address of `mydata`, line 11 in `main`) and `yours` (which has the address of `yourdata`, line 11 in `main`) in line 27 of the `swap` function. It also tracks the values of `mydata` and `yourdata` before the function call (line12), just after the function call and entry into `swap`, but before the swap (line 28), just after the swap (line 34), and after returning to `main` (to line 15).

In this example the pointers do not change their original values (addresses of int variables), but in any C++ program they could be changed in any one of several ways:

```
int* newPointer;
newPointer = NULL;          //newPointer set to NULL (no address)
newPointer = mypointer;     //newPointer set to the current value of
                            //mypointer
newPointer = &yourdata;     //newPointer set to the address of the int
                            //yourdata
```

```
newPointer = new int;       //newPointer set to point to a newly
                            allocated //integer variable
                            with no name (dynamic //allocation)
```

Any of these updates to a pointer value can be traced using a `cout` statement before and after the update. Note that the actual addresses in the example in Fig. 4.2 (output lines 2 and 6) are shown with very strange values (a mixture of letters and numbers) due to the special format used to accommodate many millions of addresses. The actual format of the addresses is not as important as the values of the addresses. For instance in the example, the address of `int mydata` is shown as `0x073f7a3c` and the value of the pointer `mine` is also shown as `0x073f7a3c`. Therefore we know that the pointer `mine` in the swap function contains the address of `mydata` in `main`, which is what it is supposed to do, and hence our trace verifies that the program is working correctly. Pointers that have been set incorrectly should be quickly detected by the trace display so corrective action can be taken.

4.3.1 A Common Error in Using Pointers

A common error that occurs in the use of pointers is when the programmer attempts to access a dynamic variable which no longer exists. Consider the following program:

```
#include <iostream>
using namespace std;

int main ()
{
    int* mypointer;

    mypointer = new int;   // allocate space for a dynamic int variable
    *mypointer = 100;      // set that variable equal to 100

    cout << mypointer << endl << *mypointer << endl;
    delete mypointer;      // deallocates the memory space reserved for
                           // *mypointer, but does not change the value
                           // of mypointer itself

    cout << mypointer << endl << *mypointer << endl; // ERROR

    cout << endl << "finished" << endl;      // this line may never
                                             // execute
```

```
    return 0;
}
```

When this program is run, the first output line will print values for `mypointer` and `*mypointer` as we would expect from the previous discussion. The second output line causes an error to occur. The problem is that while `mypointer` still contains the same address it did earlier, the dynamic variable we created no longer exists.

Note that this error can present itself in different ways on different platforms, and even on the same platform differently on different runs. On some systems, the program may halt (a `runtime` error) and you may see a printed error message such as "Bus Error" or "Segmentation Fault." On other systems, there may be no error message and the computer may even just `hang`, or the program may run to completion, and you may see a very odd value printed out for `*mypointer` by the second output line. The essence of this error is that the program has tried to access a memory location that it is not allowed to access.

4.4 STRUCTS

An *array* is a collection of data with the same data type and meaning, but with different values. A *struct* is like a database record with a collection of data of different data types and meanings, as well as different values. In a database (e.g. a personnel database) each person has a record. The record contains fields representing the attributes of each person such as last name, first name, middle initial, address, phone, student identification number, etc. A struct has *members* which are the variables that make up the whole struct. The members of a struct are equivalent to the fields of a database record. Structs can also be declared as arrays, with each element of the array being a single struct (or record) with all its members.

Debugging programs with structs can make use of tracing by simply displaying the values of a struct's members before and after a change is made to the struct. If we are dealing with an array of structs, then individual structs (or elements) of the array can be displayed before and after changes are made to them; or if there are many changes in the array, the entire array can be displayed.

In Fig. 4.3 we see a simple program involving a 100-element struct array for regional gas station data. Each struct has five members that hold, respectively, the station identification number, the week, the gas type, the gas price for that gas type, and the gallons sold that week. The program shows how the first two records (first two elements in the struct array) might be initialized (lines 30-43), and we assume the data for the other 98 records has been read in from external files (line 45). The program then computes the total sales of gas for each type of gas from all the gas stations in the region (lines 51-63). Finally the program displays the individual data values for each record (lines 65-66).

The tracing code to help verify the program computations is shown in boldface. The function prototype `void PrintRecord` appears in line 17 for the display of a single struct (all its members), and the function itself appears in lines 70-76. The calls to the trace function `PrintRecord` are shown in the code (lines 36-37 and 47-48) just after the first record is initialized and again just after the second record is initialized. The output for these two traces is shown in lines 1-7 in Fig. 4.4

```
/*Debugging Example - This program illustrates the use of tracing to
display changes in structs during the execution of the program. */

1 #include <iostream>
2 #include <iomanip>
3 #include <string>
4 using namespace std;
5
6 const int MAX_NO_RECORDS = 100;
7
8 struct GasStation
9 {
10     int station_id;
11     int week;
12     string gass_type;
13     float gas_price;
14     float gallons_sold;
15 };
16
17 void PrintRecord (int, GasStation); //function prototype to display
                                         //one struct
18 void PrintRecords (const GasStation[]);  //function prototype to
                                              //display struct array
19
20 int main()
21 {
22     double sales_regular = 0.;
23     double sales_supreme = 0.;
24     double sales_diesel = 0.;
25     int i;
26
27    GasStation my_station[MAX_NO_RECORDS];
```

Figure 4.3

Example program for testing structs

```

// initialization of first my_station record
my_station[0].station_id = 1;
            my_station[0].week = 1;
            my_station[0].gas_type = "Regular";
            my_station[0].gas_price = 205.9;
            my_station[0].gallons_sold = 5216.3;

//trace to display the first my_station record
PrintRecord (1, my_station[0]);

//initialization of second my_station record using
//struct assignment and changes
my_station[1] = my_station[0];
my_station[1].week = 2;
my_station[1].gas_price = 207.9;
my_station[1].gallons_sold = 7311.9;

//insert code to read in data for the other 98 records

//trace to display the second my_station record
PrintRecord (2, my_station[1]);

//To get the total sales for each type of gas, do this
for (i = 0; i < MAX_NO_RECORDS; i++)
{
   if (my_station[i].gas_type == "Regular")
     sales_regular = sales_regular +
     my_station[i].gas_price*my_station[i].gallons_sold;
   else if (my_station[i].gas_type == "Supreme")
     sales_supreme = sales_supreme +
     my_station[i].gas_price*my_station[i].gallons_sold;
   else if (my_station[i].gas_type == "Diesel")
     sales_diesel = sales_diesel +
     my_station[i]gas_price*my_station[i].gallions_sold;
   else
```

Figure 4.3 (Continued)

```
      cout << "Error - wrong type of gas in array element:" << i;
   }
cout << "Total Regular gas sales in the region = $" << fixed
      << setprecision(2);
cout << sales_regular/100 << endl << endl;

// display all my_station records
PrintRecords (my_station);
return 0;
}

   void PrintRecord (int loc, GasStation this_station)
   {

      cout << "GAS STATION STATISTICS - Location No. " << loc << endl;
      cout << " station_id week gas_type gas_price
              gallons_sold" << endl;
      cout << "this_station" << setw(4) << this_station.station_id
           << setw(8) << this_station.week << setw(12)
           << this_station.gas_type
           << setw(10) << this_station.gas_price << setw(14)
           << this_station.gallons_sold << endl << endl;
   }

   void PrintRecords (const GasStation my_station[])
   {
      int i;
      cout << "STATISTICS FROM EACH GAS STATION IN THE REGION"
           << endl;
      cout << "station_id week gas_type gas_price
              gallons_sold" << endl;
      for (i = 0; i < MAX_NO_RECORDS; i++)
      {
      cout << "my_station [" << i << "]" << setw(4)
           << my_station[i].station_id << setw (8)
           << my_station[i].week << setw(12)
           << my_station[i].gas_type
```

Figure 4.3 (Continued)

```
              << setw(10) << my_station[i].gas_price << setw(14)
              << my_station[i].gallons_sold << endl;
        }
}
```

Figure 4.3 (Continued)

Fig. 4.4 shows the trace statement output, followed by the computation of the total Regular gas sales in the region (line 9) and a partial display of the entire struct array as part of the normal output of the program (lines 11-21).

```
1 GAS STATION STATISTICS - Location No. 1
2   station_id week gas_type gas_price gallons_sold
3            1    1   Regular    205.9      5216.3
4
5 GAS STATION STATISTICS - Location No. 2
6   station_id week gas_type gas_price gallons_sold
7            1    2   Regular    207.9      7311.9
8
9 Total Regular gas sales in the region = $25941.80
10
11 STATISTICS FROM EACH GAS STATION IN THE REGION
12  station_id      week  gas_type     gas_price     gallons_sold
13 my_station[0]   1   1   Regular        205.9          5216.3
14 my_station[1]   1   2   Regular        208.9          7311.9
15 my_station[2]   1   1   Supreme        215.9           514.9
16 my_station[3]   1   2   Supreme        218.9           489.0
17 my_station[4]   2   1   Regular        200.9          4009.4
18 my_station[5]   2   2   Regular        203.9          3897.2
19 my_station[6]   2   1   Supreme        210.9           676.7
20 .........
21 my_station[99] 21   5   Diesel         153.9          1265.4
```

Figure 4.4 Partial output from the example program to test structs

4.5 CLASSES

Classes in C++ are the basic construct for object-oriented programming. In this section we illustrate with a simple class definition `GasStation` the use of tracing to verify the correctness of intermediate results from a computation involving classes. In the program shown in Figure 4.5 we use the same gas station example that we used for structs in Sec. 4.4, except that `GasStation` is now a class consisting of arrays for each member to represent the different records in the database to keep track of gas sales. In this case we restrict ourselves to two records for purposes of illustration, and we use tracing for all the display of record values from the `GasStation` objects (lines 18 for the prototype and 48 for the function call, and 52-58 for the public print function of `GasStation`). The tracing code and output are again shown in boldface type.

```
1 #include <iostream>
2 #include <iomanip>
3 #include <string>
4 using namespace std;
5
6 const int MAX_NO_RECS = 2; //global constant for the size
                             //of arrays in class GasStation
7
8 class GasStation
9 {
10     public:
11     int station_id[MAX_NO_RECS];
12     int week[MAX_NO_RECS];
13     string gas_type[MAX_NO_RECS];
14     float gas_price[MAX_NO_RECS];
15     float gallons_sold[MAX_NO_RECS];
16
17     void InitializeRecords();        //prototype to initialize
18     void PrintRecord(int, int);  //trace prototype
19     void PrintRecords(int);  //prototype to display
20     double ComputeSales();   //prototype to compute total sales

21
22 };
23
24 int main()
25 {
26     double sales_regular = 0.;
27     GasStation my_station;    //create new gas station object
```

Figure 4.5

Example program for testing simple classes

```
        my_station.InitializeRecords();    //initialize
        sales_regular = my_station.ComputeSales();
        cout << "Total Regular gas sales in the region = $"
             << fixed << setprecision(2)
             << sales_regular << endl << endl;
             //display all my_station records
             my_station.PrintRecords(2);
             return 0;
}

void GasStation::InitializeRecords()
{
             int i;
             for (i = 0; i < MAX_NO_RECS; i++)
             {
                 cout << "Please input gas station parameters - id,
                 week,
                 gas type, price, gallons sold: " << endl;

                 cin >> station_id[i] >> week[i] >> gas_type[i]
                 >> gas_price[i] >> gallons_sold[i];

                 //trace to display the gas station object
                 PrintRecord(i,1);
}
}
//Trace function for a single GasStation record
void GasStation::PrintRecord(int i, int loc)
{

             cout << endl << "GAS STATION STATISTICS - Location No. "
                  << loc << endl;
             cout << " station_id week gas_type gas_price
                  gallons_sold" << endl;
             cout << "this_station" << setw(5) << station_id[i]
                  << setw(8)<\n><< week[i] << setw(12)
```

Figure 4.5 (Continued)

```
                 << gas_type[i] << setw(10) << gas_price[i]
                 << setw(14) << gallons_sold[i<\n><< endl << endl;
}

void GasStation::PrintRecords(int loc)
{
            int i;
            cout << "STATISTICS FROM EACH GAS STATION - Location No. "
                 << loc << endl;
            cout << " station_id week gas_type gas_price
            gallons_sold" << endl;

            for (i = 0; i < MAX_NO_RECS; i++)
            {
                Cout << "my_station[" << i << "]" << setw(4)
                     << station_id[i] << setw(8) << week[i]
                     << setw(12) << gas_type[i] << setw(10)
                     << gas_price[i] << setw(14)
                     << gallons_sold[i] << endl;
            }
}

double GasStation::ComputeSales()
={
            int i;
            double sales_regular = 0.;

            for (i = 0; i < MAX_NO_RECS; i++)
            {
                if (gas_type[i] == "Regular")
                    sales_regular = sales_regular +
                    gas_price[i]*gallons_sold[i];
            }

return sales_regular/100;
}
```

Figure 4.5 (Continued)

The output from execution of the program in Fig. 4.5 is shown in Fig. 4.6. The normal output shows the computation of total sales of Regular gas, and the rest is trace output in boldface type. Note that the tracing includes the location number of the trace so code and output can be easily connected.

```
Please input gas station parameters - id, week, gas type, price,
gallons sold:
1 1 Regular 205.9 5216.3
GAS STATION STATISTICS - Location No. 1
    station_id     week       gas_type    gas_price          gallons_sold
this_station 1      1          Regular     205.9               5216.3

Please input gas station parameters - id, week, gas type, price,
gallons sold:
1 2 Regular 167.9 7311.9
GAS STATION STATISTICS - Location No. 1
    station_id     week       gas_type    gas_price          gallons_sold
this_station 1      2          Regular     207.9               7311.9

Total Regular gas sales in the region = $25941.80

STATISTICS FROM EACH GAS STATION - Location No. 2
    station_id     week       gas_type    gas_price          gallons_sold
my_station[0] 1     1          Regular     205.9               5216.3
my_station[1] 1     2          Regular     207.9               7311.9
```

Figure 4.6 Output from the example program to test classes

This completes our discussion of the use of tracing to debug the more common C++ constructs. In the next chapter we focus on using the interactive debugger, an even more powerful tool.

CHAPTER 5

Using an Interactive Debugger

5.1 CHAPTER OBJECTIVES

- To be able to identify the fundamental commands and tools provided in modern interactive debuggers
- To be able to apply these tools to the debugging and testing of a simple C++ program
- To carefully study an example of an interactive debugging task using the Metrowerks CodeWarrior and Microsoft Visual C++ compilers

5.2 FUNDAMENTALS

In Chapters 3 and 4, you learned how to find and correct program bugs by tracing your program's behavior using extra printing statements. In this chapter, you will learn to use an additional tool, the *interactive debugger*. Note that these two tools can be used either separately or together in your work. They share the fundamental goals of pinpointing the locations where program errors occur and discovering what the errors are, while, of course, helping you correct those errors.

An interactive debugger allows you to examine the behavior of your C++ program while it is running. A debugger can be an invaluable aid in correcting errors in your code. This chapter will describe common tools available in typical modern interactive debugging systems.

The essential idea behind interactive debugging is to discover *critical points* in your program where errors occur. To do this, you can stop execution at various statements in the program and look at the values of *critical variables*. While the run is suspended, you are able to look at a *snapshot* of your program's activity. Execution can then be resumed at the point at which the program run was stopped. In addition, you may observe the program's execution in order to check its *flow of control.*

When you check the values of *critical variables* —those you believe to be important in causing your program's problems, the debugger will tell you what values the variables *actually* hold. This may not be the same as what you *want* them to hold or *think* they *should* hold! If the value of some variable is not what you expected, search for the reasons for the incorrect value. Was it read as input incorrectly, or calculated incorrectly, or not passed back from a subprogram correctly, or something else?

The *flow of control* in a program is the order in which the program's statements are executed. You can observe this flow by running the program under the control of the debugger, which is capable both of executing one statement at a time and of executing groups of statements all at once. At all points the debugger displays a pointer to the statement that is to be executed next. Is the flow of control what you think it should be? Look for dangling `elses`, missing or out-of-order subprogram calls, infinite loops and other errors.

We recommend that you refer to Appendix B.2 for the checklist that helps you identify critical variables and important locations in your program's flow of control.

In a typical modern Integrated Development Environment (IDE), you will find that the language compiler is one part of the system, and that the interactive debugger is another part. To debug your program using the debugger, you must specifically *run* the interactive debugger, which is itself a program. Then, you can run the C++ program you are working on by choosing the appropriate command from within the debugging program's menus. In this situation, you are running your C++ program under the control of the interactive debugger. The debugger allows you to observe the behavior of your C++ program as it runs.

In this discussion, we will assume that your debugger provides a typical graphical user interface (GUI), using windows and various graphical items to display information for you. Note that if you are using a text-based debugger (such as dbx on a UNIX machine), you will still find that the debugging commands and tasks described in this chapter illustrated with examples using graphics-based debuggers are applicable to your work with a text-based debugger. This is because all debuggers provide essentially the same capabilities, whether graphics based or text based.

In sections 5.3 through 5.6, we study the use of interactive debugging techniques to debug a small example program. General debugging tools are discussed throughout the chapter. In sections 5.3 and 5.4, we specifically study the use of the Metrowerks CodeWarrior Development Studio for Windows version 9 interactive debugger. In sections 5.5 and 5.6, we study the same tasks using the Microsoft Visual C++ 6.0 interactive debugger. We recommend that you read the sections corresponding to the compiler you are using. If you are using another compiler, it will still be helpful to read one of these sections because modern IDEs are all very similar.

5.3 DEBUGGING WITH METROWERKS CODEWARRIOR

5.3.1 Initiating the Debugging Process

The first step involves initiating your C++ program's execution, under the control of the debugger. In CodeWarrior, you would choose Debug from the Project menu to begin this step. This command will load your program into memory so that it is ready to start executing under the debugger's control.

Graphics-based IDEs display your program and the debugging information you need in one or more windows on your screen. After you have started running your C++ program, one or more new windows typically appear. One window will display the C++ program, and include an arrow that points to the next statement to be executed. We will call this window the *program window*, and the arrow, the *current statement indicator*. You will also see a list of variables that are defined in the currently executing portion of your program.

Figure 5.1 shows an example of Codewarrior's main debugging window.

In the list of variables, you will see the names of variables you have declared, and as the C++ program actually runs, you will see the current values of these

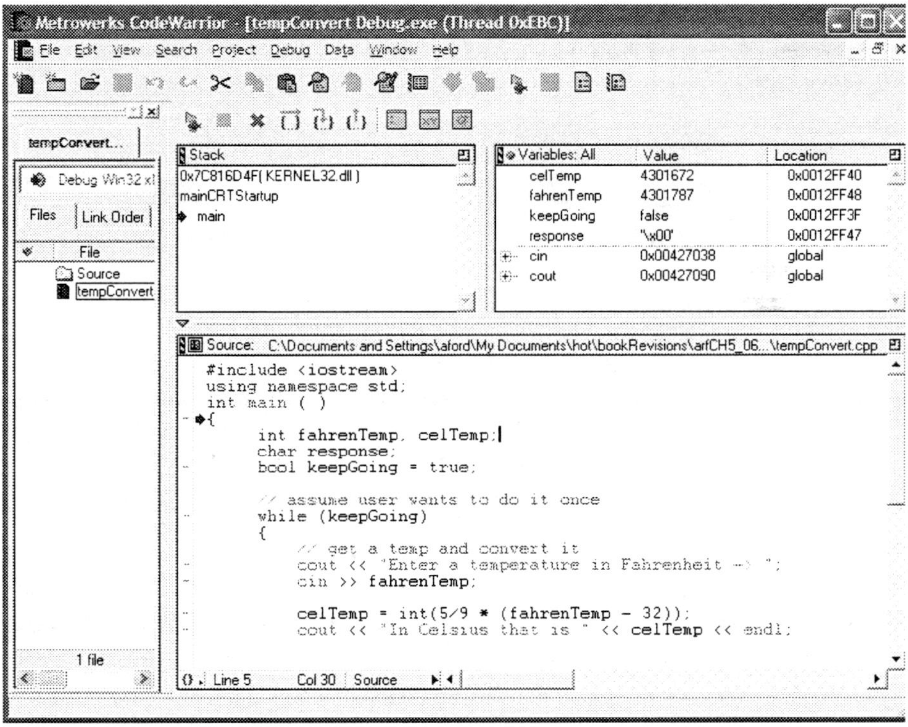

Figure 5.1

CodeWarrior's main debugging window

variables displayed. A variable having no current value is *undefined* or *uninitialized*, and you will typically see some random value displayed in its place. The variables you see are primarily *local* variables—that is, those declared in the currently executing function, main.

In addition, most systems will show a list of the currently active functions, in an order that shows the *call chain*, or order in which the calls occurred. For example, if during a run, the main function called function `ProcessValues`, and `ProcessValues` called function `ReadOneItem`, you would see this list as the call chain:

```
main
ProcessValues
ReadOneItem
```

The call chain is also often called a *stack trace*. In CodeWarrior, we see this call chain in the upper left windowpane, listed under "Stack."

5.3.2 Running Your C++ Program Under Control of the Debugger

After you have activated the debugger by choosing Debug under the Project menu, your C++ program is stored in memory and is ready to execute under the debugger's control. The debugger is called *interactive* because you, the programmer, can at any time tell the debugger to display certain values or alter the flow of control of the program.

Some of the fundamental commands are:

Kill The Kill command will completely halt execution of your C++ program and return control to the debugger program.

Restart The Restart command will stop the current execution of your program and restart it from the beginning.

Step Commands A Step command allows you to execute one statement. The statement that executes when you select Step is the one pointed at by the current statement indicator. After this single statement is executed, program execution will be suspended again, and you may look at variables or enter another debugging command. Using Step, you can observe the effect that one statement has on your program's behavior. Variations of step include:

Step Over Function Calls Step Over allows one statement to execute, and if that one statement is a function call, the entire function will execute, leaving the current statement indicator at the statement *after* the function call. In other words, you will not see the current statement indicator move through the statements that are inside the called function.

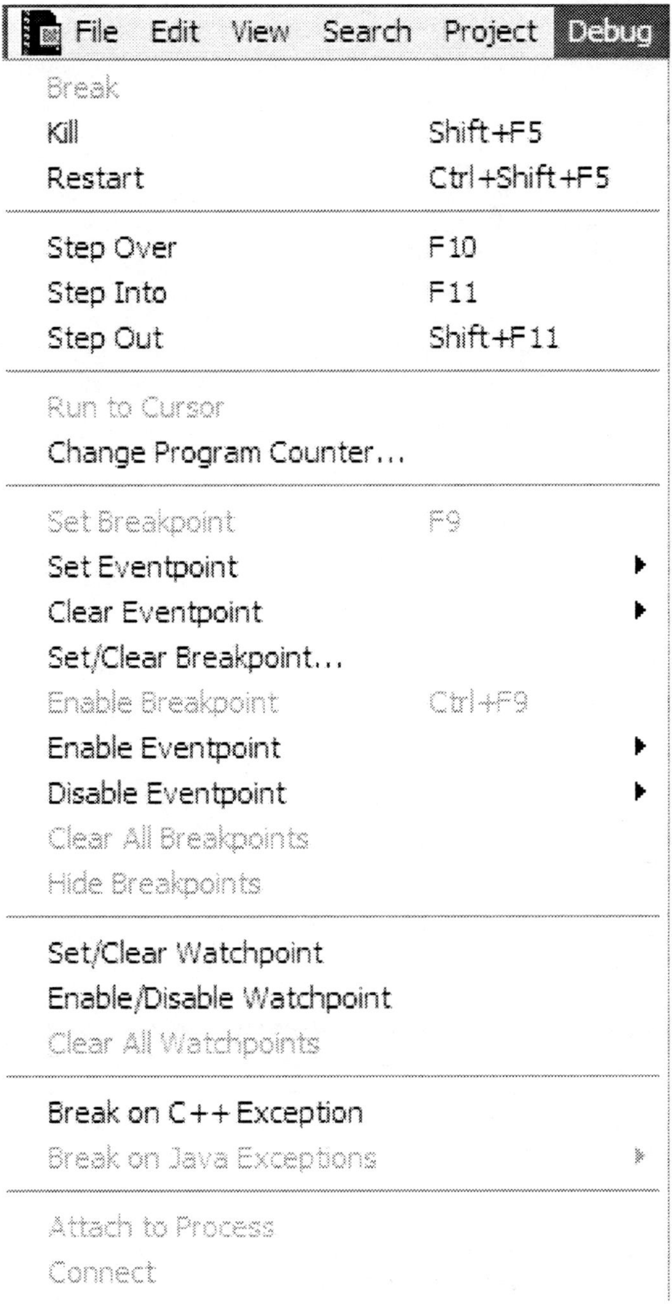

Figure 5.2

Debug menu in CodeWarrior

Step Into Function Calls Step Into also allows one statement to execute, but if that one statement is a function call, the current statement indicator will actually enter that function. Using Step Into, you may enter a called function and then execute that function's statements one at a time.

Note that if you Step Into a standard function such as cout, you may see the actual source C++ code for `cout`, or sometimes its equivalent assembly language translation, in your program window. It is generally preferable to Step Over standard functions rather than to enter them.

Step Out of a Function Step Out causes the current statement indicator to exit from a function in which you currently are operating. The function will finish executing, and then you will see the current statement indicator move to the statement in the caller, just after the call to the function you just exited.

In CodeWarrior, the Step commands provided are Step Over, Step Into, and Step Out, and are found in the Debug menu as shown above.

As you execute your code using the debugger, keep in mind that your primary focus should be on examining the values of critical variables and observing the program's flow of control. The overall goal, of course, is to discover points in the program at which errors occur.

5.3.3 A Note on Infinite Loops

If your program contains an infinite loop, you can easily detect it using Step commands. As you step through the code, at some point you will see the program get stuck inside some loop. In this situation the current statement arrow will just keep going through the same code over and over, indefinitely. In this case, use the Kill command to completely halt the C++ program's execution.

5.3.4 Using Breakpoints

Sometimes even stepping with Step Over Function Calls will be too slow. You then may want to run your program at normal speed up to a certain point, then stop it and check the values of critical variables at that point. *Breakpoints* are specific statement(s) at which you want execution to be suspended.

To insert a breakpoint in your code, you typically click on the statement at which you want execution to stop, or on some indicator next to that statement. For example, in CodeWarrior, you click on the gray line beside a statement. The line will become a *red* full circle, indicating that the breakpoint is *set*. Now when you run the program under the debugger's control, execution will automatically halt at this breakpoint.

You can insert as many breakpoints as you like, but only in front of executable C++ statements, not at comments, declarations, and so on.

To remove a breakpoint in CodeWarrior, click on the full red circle so that it becomes a flat gray line again. To remove all breakpoints simultaneously, select Clear All Breakpoints from the Debug menu.

To run a program at normal speed until a breakpoint is encountered, choose Debug from the CodeWarrior's Project menu. Once the program has been interrupted by a breakpoint, you can resume execution or debug using any of the commands described earlier. The Step commands may prove particularly useful once you have suspended execution at a breakpoint.

5.3.5 Changing the Value of a Variable "On the Fly"

By actually altering the value of the variable during the run, using the debugger, you can answer questions such as, "What if the variable X did have the correct value of 2.3 instead of this wrong value it has now?" Your debugger probably will provide some means of doing this. In CodeWarrior, double-click on the value of the variable you want to change. Then, just type in the new value you want to use. When you resume execution, the variable will have the value you just typed in.

5.3.6 Function Pop-Up Menus

Most IDEs provide some method of easily selecting a particular function's code to display in the program window. For example, if the main function is currently displayed in the program window, but you want to look at function `MyFunc`, you can tell the debugger to bring `MyFunc` into the program window. In CodeWarrior, if you click on the { } displayed at the bottom left of the program window, you will see a pop-up menu of the names of the functions contained in your program, in their order of declaration. If you then select a particular function in the list, it will immediately be displayed in the program window.

5.3.7 Viewing Data Types

Data types (such as `int`, `double`, etc.) are usually not displayed alongside the names of variables in your debugger's windows, although most debuggers will allow you to choose to see the data types. In CodeWarrior, you can tell the debugger to show you the data types that correspond to displayed variables by clicking on a variable to highlight it, and then choosing Show Types from the Data menu.

5.3.8 Displaying Values in a Structured Type Variable

The values inside of structured variables such as arrays, structs, and classes are typically not all displayed in the debugger's window, unless you specifically choose to have them displayed. In CodeWarrior, to see all of the values in a structured variable, you must click on the small plus symbol to the left of the variable's name. You will see the values displayed just after the name of the variable. As an alternative, you can double-click on the variable name itself, and the values of its components will be displayed in a new window.

Note that many debuggers, as a default, will display only the memory address of the first element in a structured variable. This can be useful debugging information as well, depending on what your program needs to do.

5.3.9 Compiler and Debugger Preferences

Most compilers allow you to alter preferences that significantly affect the behavior of the debugger. Look for a Preferences menu item, usually found under the Edit menu, to find what debugging options you have available in your local system.

For example, CodeWarrior allows you to select a preference that will cause the names of variables that have just changed to be displayed in a highlight color of your choice.

5.4 EXAMPLE: DEBUGGING A SAMPLE C++ PROGRAM USING METROWERKS CODEWARRIOR

In this section, we will look at a short C++ program containing a few bugs. Using the interactive debugger provided in Metrowerks CodeWarrior as an example, we will trace through the steps a programmer would go through in order to discover what is wrong in the program and then to fix it appropriately. The figures we show to illustrate the state of the debugger at various points were produced by CodeWarrior and are in fact screen shots of its debugging windows. Other modern compiler systems provide similar features.

The C++ program we will consider is intended to repeatedly read in Fahrenheit temperatures from the user, and convert each to its equivalent Celsius value. After each temperature is converted, the user is asked whether he or she would like to convert another temperature. The process is supposed to repeat until the user indicates that he or she does not want to enter any more temperature values.

5.4.1 Sample C++ Program: Buggy Version

Consider the following initial version of the program, which produces no syntax errors or warnings:

```
#include <iostream>
using namespace std;
int main ( )
{
   int fahrenTemp, celTemp;
   char response;
   bool keepGoing = true;

   // assume user wants to do it once
   while (keepGoing)
   {
       // get a temp and convert it
       cout << "Enter a temperature in Fahrenheit -> ";
       cin >> fahrenTemp;
```

```
        celTemp = int(5/9 * (fahrenTemp - 32));
        cout << "In Celsius that is " << celTemp << endl;

        // ask if user wants to convert another
        cout << endl
             << "Do you want to enter another temperature?"
             << " Enter y or n -> ";
        cin >> response;

        // input error checking
        while ((response != y) || (response != n))
        {
        cout << "Please try again. Enter y or n -> ";
        cin >> response;
        }

        // reset flag
        keepGoing = (response == y);
    }

    return 0;
}       // end of main
```

As we run this program, we may begin to lose patience and perhaps our faith in computers, when we observe the following output dialogue:

```
Enter a temperature in Fahrenheit -> 75
In Celsius that is 0

Do you want to enter another temperature? Enter y or n -> y
Please try again. Enter y or n -> y
Please try again. Enter y or n -> y
Please try again. Enter y or n -> y
Please try again. Enter y or n -> n
Please try again. Enter y or n ->
```

We have to forcibly quit the program by clicking on the X in the upper right corner of the program's output window in order to end this misery. We then decide to use the interactive debugger to help us figure out what's wrong. The next few sections illustrate this process.

5.4.2 Sample C++ Program: Using Step to Find the 1st Error

In the previous section, we saw that the calculation of the Celsius temperature produced an incorrect value of 0 for a Fahrenheit value of 75. There are two critical variables here, the first of which is `fahrenTemp`. It is possible that `fahrenTemp` is somehow not being read as input and stored in memory correctly. The second critical variable is `celTemp` itself. It may not be calculated correctly. Let's check both by using the debugger to step through the program, one statement at a time, up to the point just before `celTemp's` value is output.

Figure 5.3 shows the CodeWarrior debugger's program window right at the point of execution of the program. In the windowpane labeled "Stack," we see the call chain. Function `main` is the only active function we are concerned with here. In the pane labeled "Variables" we see the four variables we have declared, `celTemp, fahrenTemp, keepGoing` and `response`. At this point the values for all of those variables are not meaningful, because those variables are not initialized, just containing whatever random information happens to be in their memory locations. In the pane labeled "Source" we see our C++ source program, with the current statement indicator shown as an arrow, pointing at the next statement to be executed. Note that at the beginning of the run, it points to the first brace of `main`.

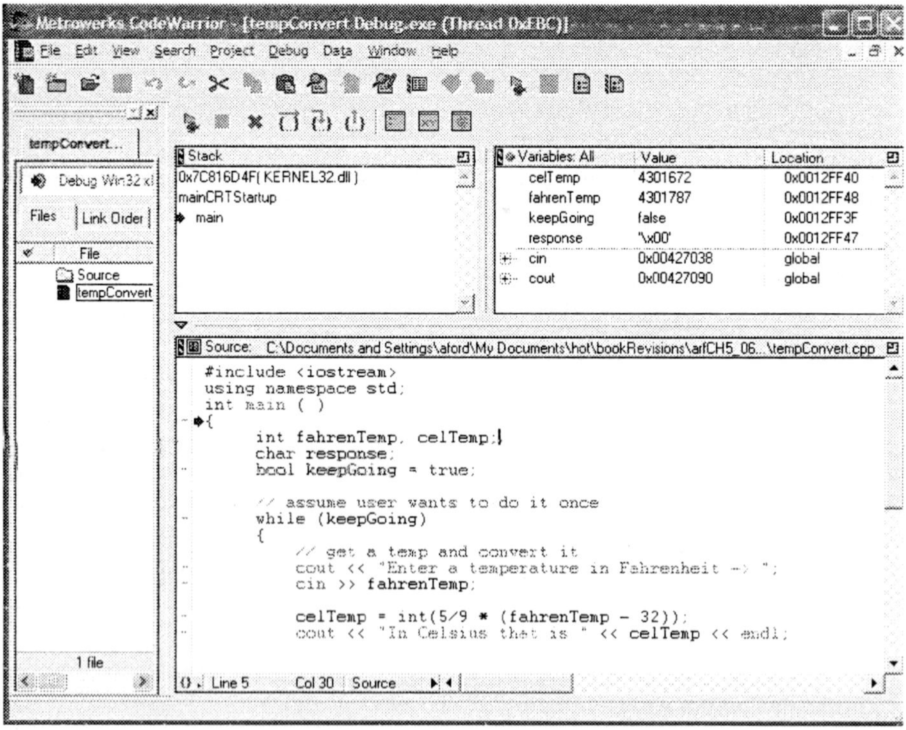

Figure 5.3

Debugging window at initial state

We next use the Step Over command to execute the next few lines, bringing us to the state shown in Figure 5.4. Figure 5.4 shows the current statement indicator at the output statement for `celTemp`. This means that we have already entered a value for `fahrenTemp` (75), and can check the variables pane to see if it is correct. It is correct, so `fahrenTemp` is not the problem. We next look at `celTemp`. It is 0, which we know is wrong. So we can conclude that the assignment statement which calculates `celTemp` contains one or more errors.

Looking at the assignment, we notice that while the formula looks superficially correct, the value of the expression "5/9" is zero. Because we are dividing two integer values, any fractional portion of the result is simply truncated. That makes the value of the entire calculation zero. If we change "5/9" to evaluate using real number division, we can fix this one problem and see if we then get a correct result.

Using the Kill command, we stop execution, go back into our program code, and change the assignment statement so that it reads "5.0/9.0" instead of "5/9." Then, we start running the program again with Debug, and use Step Over to get to the same location.

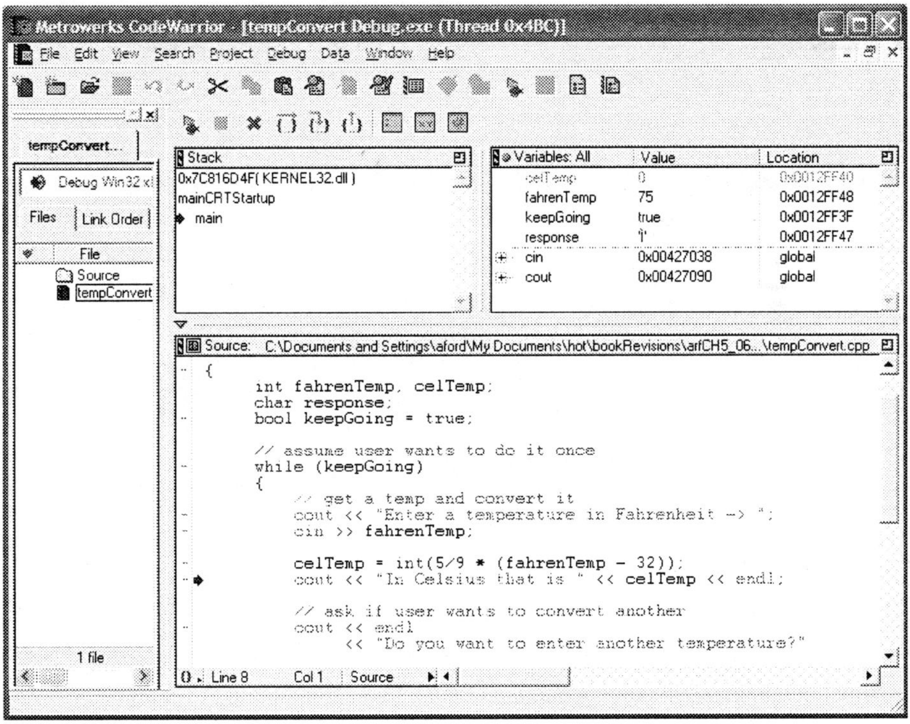

Figure 5.4

Debugging window at output line for celTemp, before correction

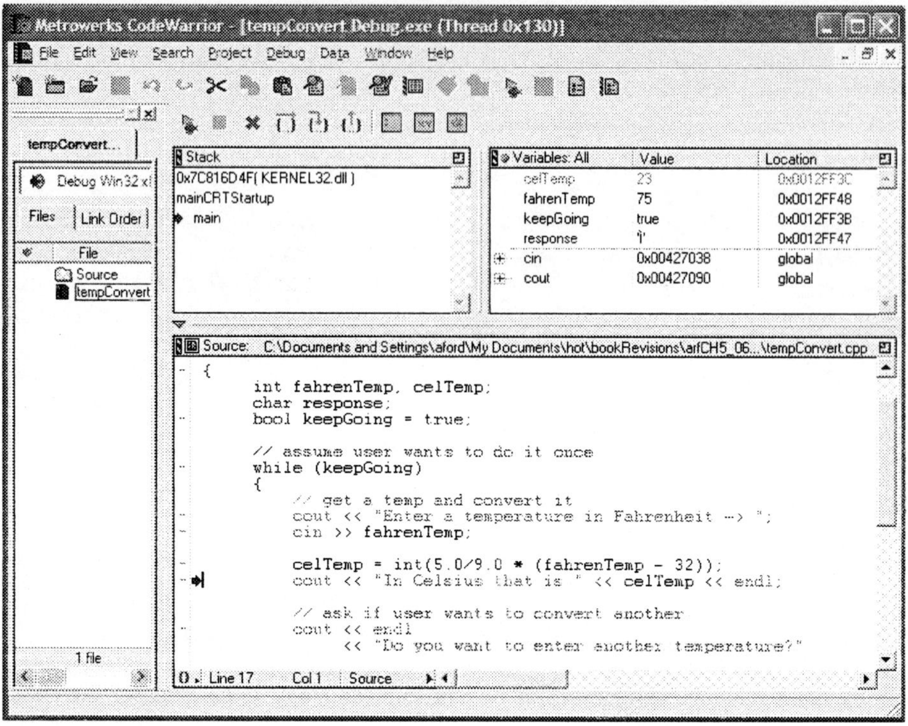

Figure 5.5

Debugging window at output line for celTemp, after correction

Figure 5.5 shows that we have solved our first problem. The value of `celTemp` is now 23, which is correct. We decide to Kill the program run and celebrate this small victory. Of course, the program must be tested with other temperature values before we know it is running correctly for all possible values.

5.4.3 Sample C++ Program: Using Breakpoints to Find the 2nd Error

We can guess from our original program output that we are stuck in an *infinite loop*, the loop in which we enter a *y* or an *n* to indicate whether we want to enter another temperature or not. There is one critical variable here, `response`.

We will set breakpoints at positions that will help us determine exactly what the problem is with this loop. There are two possible reasons the loop might be infinite: (1) `response` is not read as input and stored in memory correctly, or (2) the logical expression at the loop entrance is faulty, so that even if `response` is read and stored correctly, we remain stuck.

Figure 5.6 shows the CodeWarrior debugger's program window just at the point where we have initiated execution of the program using Debug and then chosen two breakpoints. To create a breakpoint in CodeWarrior, we click on the flattened line next to a C++ statement. The flattened line then turns into a red "stop sign," indicat-

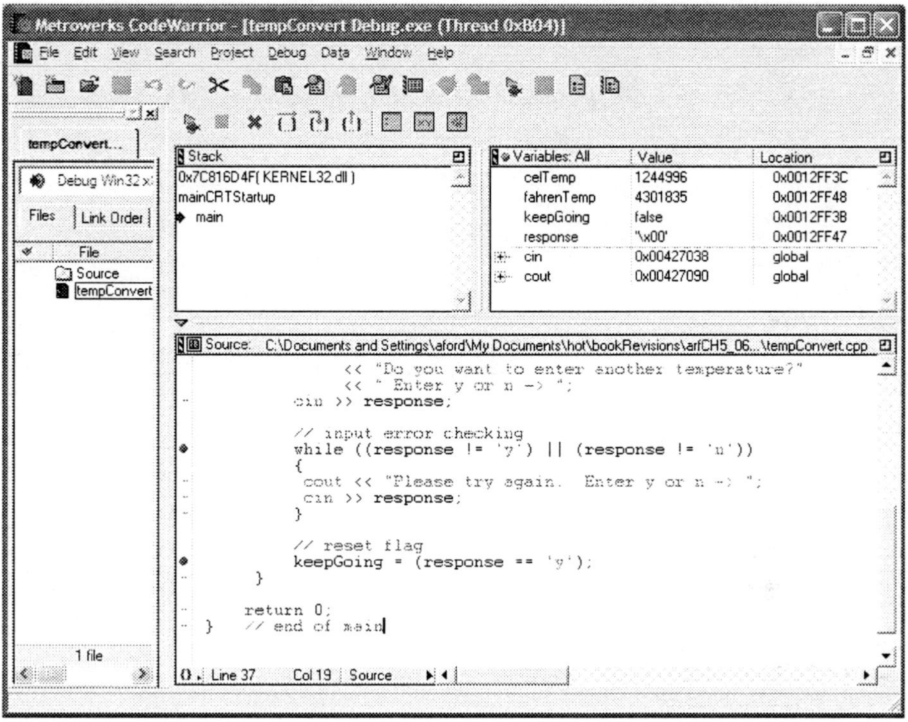

Figure 5.6

Debugging window after choosing two breakpoints

ing a breakpoint has been set. Remember execution will then stop just before the breakpoint statement executes.

We now start the program using Run under the Project menu, and it will stop execution when it hits the first breakpoint, which is just before the loop we are concerned about. Note that the program will also pause when input from the keyboard is needed. You will have to click on the black button at the bottom of the screen named C:\ to enter input. Then click on your Codewarrior window to return to debugging. Figure 5.7 shows the state of the program when we have run the program up to the first breakpoint, and then have used Step Over to find out what will happen next. Assume that we entered a *y* when asked for a response.

Looking at the variables window, we see that `response` is actually *y*, which in this case, is correct. This means `response` is being read and stored correctly. This critical variable is fine, and the loop body should not execute at all. However, the current statement indicator shows that the next statement to be executed is the `cout` call, which is inside the loop that prints a prompt for a new value. Note that if we had correctly entered an *n*, the exact same thing would have happened, indicating that we are indeed stuck in this loop. No matter what value we type in, we remain in the loop. We can also change the value of `response` "on the fly" (described earlier in this chapter)

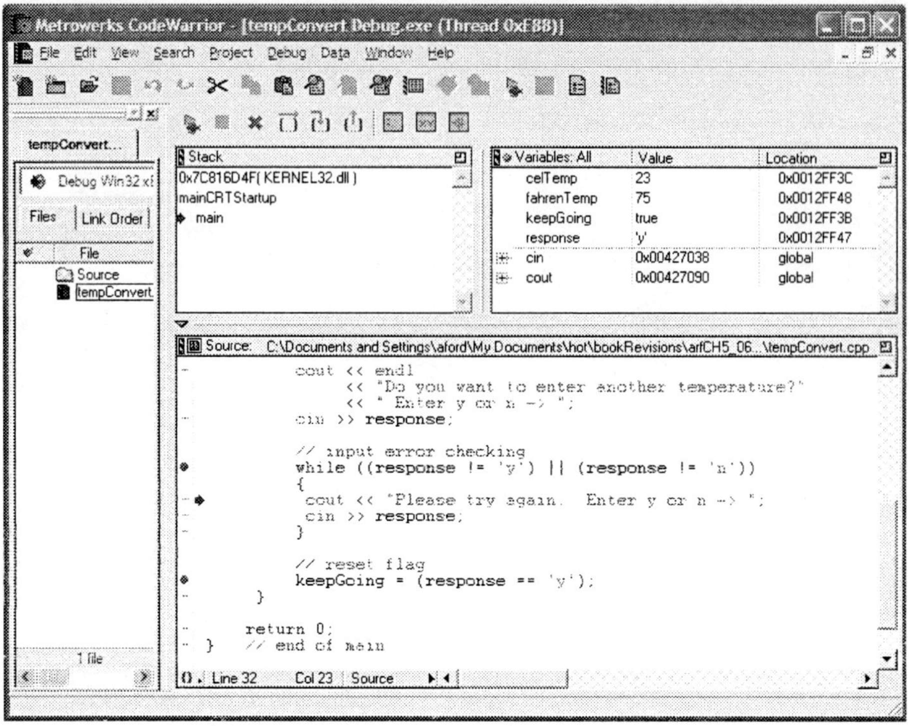

Figure 5.7

Debugging window after first breakpoint

to whatever value we want to check. We note if we tried repeatedly entering values for `response`, we would see that the current statement indicator would *never* reach the 2nd breakpoint that we set. The flow of control simply cannot get to that point in the program.

So, how should we proceed? The only possibility left is that the logical expression controlling the loop is wrong. Indeed, you may recall from Chapter 2 that the expression

```
(response != y) || (response != n)
```

is always *true*, regardless of the value of `response`. This is why the loop can never exit. Realizing this, we can Kill the program, change the expression to the correct version,

```
(response != y) && (response != n)
```

and run the program again. After this change, the program works correctly!

Figure 5.8 shows that once the logical expression has been corrected, the flow of control does indeed proceed to the 2nd breakpoint we set, where the variable

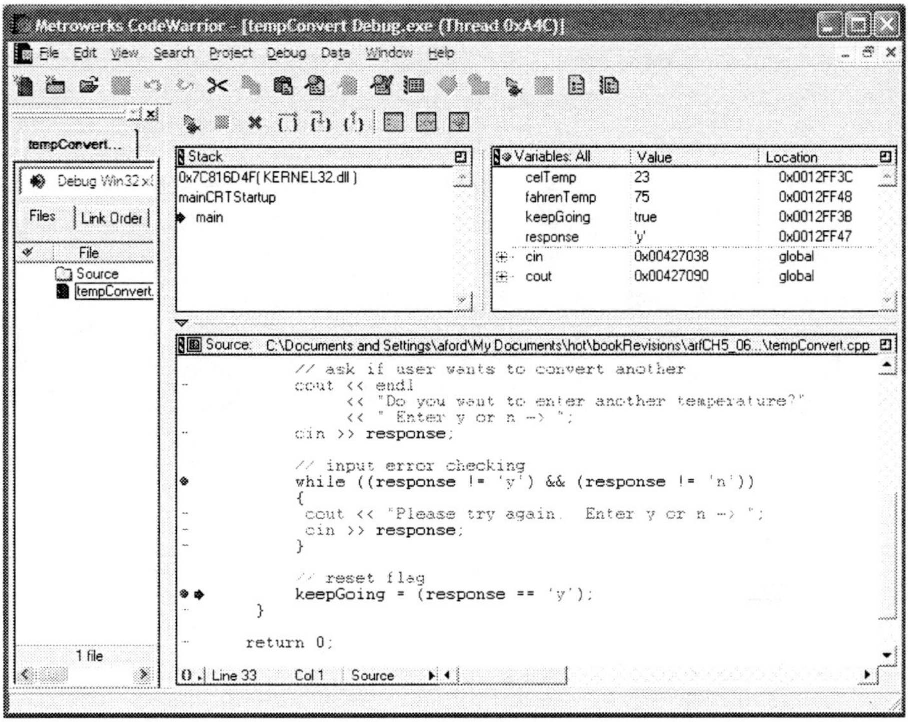

Figure 5.8

Debugging window at second breakpoint

`keepGoing` is assigned a value. We can now stop at this point, do one Step Over, and check that `keepGoing` is being set correctly to true (1) or false (0).

We have exited the infinite loop and successfully corrected the program. At this point it is important to continue to test the program thoroughly with different input values and input combinations, to verify that the entire program does work correctly for all possible inputs.

5.4.4 Sample C++ Program: Corrected Version

The following shows the corrected program in its entirety:

```
#include <iostream>
using namespace std;
int main ( )
{
    int fahrenTemp, celTemp;
    char response;
    bool keepGoing = true;
```

```
    // assume user wants to do it once
    while (keepGoing)
    {
        // get a temp and convert it
        cout << "Enter a temperature in Fahrenheit -> ";
        cin >> fahrenTemp;

        celTemp = int(5.0/9.0 * (fahrenTemp - 32));
        cout << "In Celsius that is " << celTemp << endl;

        // ask if user wants to convert another
        cout << endl
            "Do you want to enter another temperature?"
            << " Enter y or n -> ";
        cin >> response;

        // input error checking
        while ((response != y) && (response != n))
        {
            cout << "Please try again. Enter y or n -> ";
            cin >> response;
        }

        // reset flag
        keepGoing = (response == y);
    }

    return 0;
} // end of main
```

When we run this version of the program, correct output is displayed as follows:

```
Enter a temperature in Fahrenheit -> 75
In Celsius that is 23

Do you want to enter another temperature? Enter y or n -> y
Enter a temperature in Fahrenheit -> 212
In Celsius that is 100

Do you want to enter another temperature? Enter y or n -> n
```

5.5 DEBUGGING WITH MICROSOFT VISUAL C++

5.5.1 Initiating the Debugging Process

The first step in the debugging process is usually to run or activate the interactive debugger by choosing the appropriate menu item in your IDE. In Visual C++, we first go to the Build menu and choose Set Active Configurations. This will cause a dialog box to appear. In this dialog box, make sure that the highlighted line ends with Win 32 Debug. If that line is not highlighted, click on it to select it, and then click OK. In this discussion, we assume you set up your project as a *Win 32 Console Application*.

The next step involves actually initiating your C++ program's execution, under the control of the debugger. In Visual C++, you would choose Start Debug from the Build menu and then choose Step Into from the submenu that immediately appears. This command will load your program into memory and start executing your main function.

Graphics-based IDEs display your program and the debugging information you need in one or more windows on your screen. After you have started your C++ program running, you will see the Visual C++ window change. We will call the new window the *debugging window*. One pane will display the C++ program. We will call this the *program pane*.

Figure 5.9 illustrates the main debugging window of Visual C++, along with its initial Start Debug menu.

Once your program is running under the debugger, the program pane will include an arrow pointing to the next statement to be executed. We will call this the *current statement indicator*. You will also see a list of variables that are defined in the currently executing portion of your program. This list of variables will appear in the lower left pane, labeled with the word *Context*. We will call this display the *variables pane*. This pane includes tabs to select various types of variables such as auto, local, and so on. Take a look at Figure 5.12 at this time to see examples of these items.

In the list of variables, you will see the names of variables you have declared; and as the C++ program actually runs, you will see the current values of these variables. If a value is red, it has just changed. A variable having no current value is *undefined* or *uninitialized*, and you will see some random value represented in its place. {Note: some compilers, like Microsoft Visual C++ 6.0, may display a fixed constant value to represent an unitialized variable. It is beyond the scope of this text to explain why that may be done.} The variables you typically want to see are *local* variables—that is, those declared in the currently executing function.

On your lower right, you will see *the watch pane*. You can drag highlighted variables or expressions to this pane to see their values displayed there.

In addition, most systems will show a list of the currently active functions, in an order that shows the *call chain*, or order in which the calls occurred. For example, if during a run, the main function called function `ProcessValues`, and `ProcessValues` called function `ReadOneItem`, you would see this list as the call chain:

```
main

ProcessValues

ReadOneItem
```

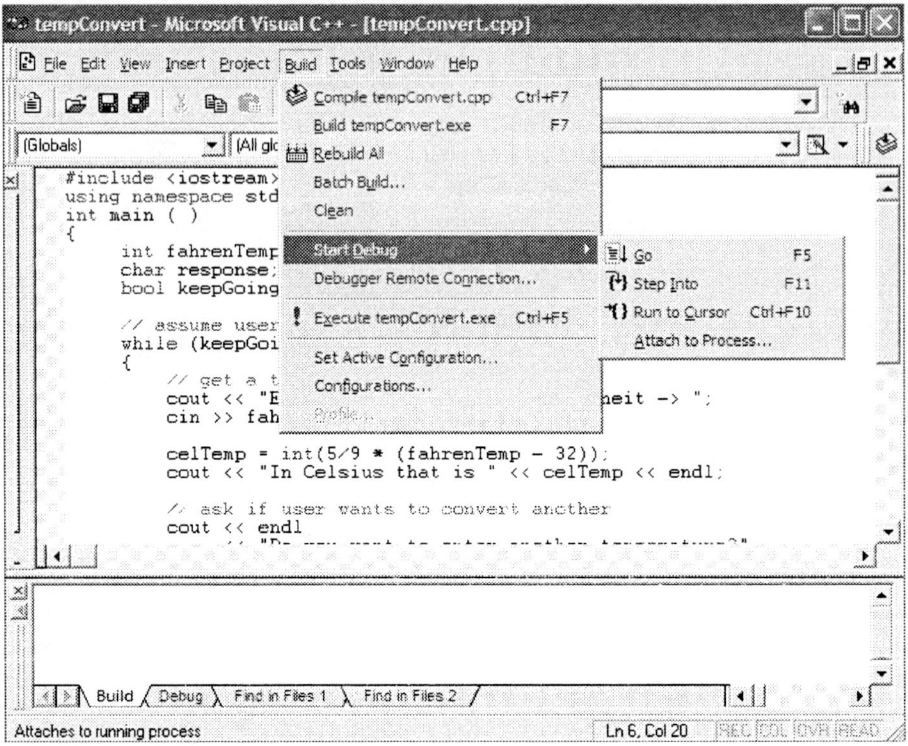

Figure 5.9

Visual C++ main debugging window and Start Debug menu

The call chain is also often called a *stack trace*. In Visual C++, we can look at the call chain by clicking on the triangle next to Context in the lower left pane.

5.5.2 Running Your C++ Program Under Control of the Debugger

After you have activated the debugger and indicated that it must now run your program, the C++ program is stored in memory and is ready to execute under the debugger's supervision. The debugger is called *interactive* because you, the programmer, can at any time tell the debugger to display certain values or alter the flow of control of the program. Commands which alter the flow of control are found in the Debug menu and in the corresponding Debug toolbar which appears when debugging.

Figure 5.10 shows you the Visual C++ Debug menu.

Figure 5.11 displays the corresponding Debug toolbar, which contains most of the same commands, but in button form.

The commands that follow are debugging commands.

Go The Go command will start actual execution of your C++ program, at the first statement in the main function. If there are no breakpoints set in the program (dis-

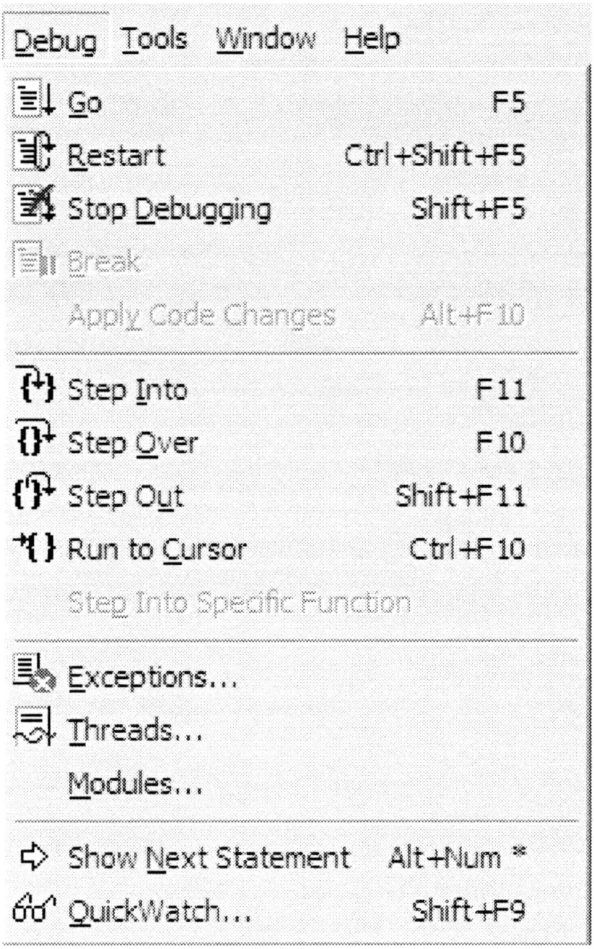

Figure 5.10

Visual C++ Debug menu

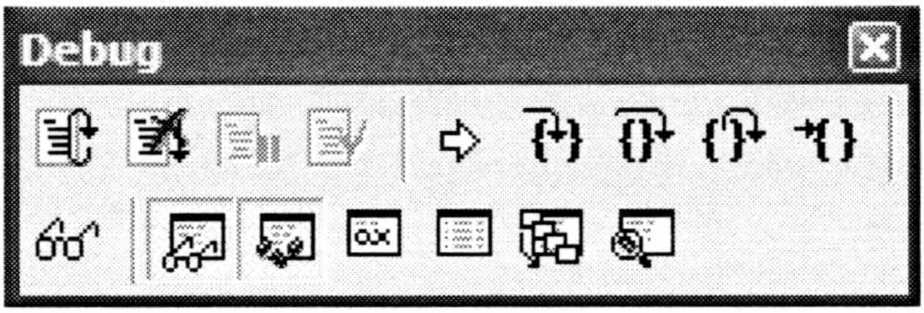

Figure 5.11

Visual C++ Debug toolbar

cussed below), execution will continue until the program either finishes or crashes. The Go command is also used to resume execution after it has been suspended by a breakpoint.

Restart The Restart command is used to re-initialize your debugging session, (i.e., start over).

Run to Cursor The Run to Cursor command can be used to execute all statements up to a particular program statement. Place the cursor on a line in the program below the line currently active. Then choose Run to Cursor.

Stop Debugging The Stop Debugging command will completely halt execution of your C++ program and return control to Visual C++.

Step Commands A Step command allows you to execute one statement. The statement that executes when you select Step is the one pointed at by the current statement indicator. After this single statement is executed, program execution will be suspended again and you may look at variables or enter another debugging command. Using Step, you can observe the effect that one statement has on your program's behavior. Variations of step include the following:

Step Over Function Calls Step Over allows one statement to execute, and if that one statement is a function call, the entire function will execute, leaving the current statement indicator at the statement *after* the function call. In other words, you will not see the current statement indicator move through the statements that are inside the called function.

Step Into Function Calls Step Into also allows one statement to execute, but if that one statement is a function call, the current statement indicator will actually enter that function. Using Step Into, you can enter a called function and then execute that function's statements one at a time if you choose.

Note that if you Step Into a standard function such as cout, you may see the actual source C++ code for cout, or sometimes its equivalent assembly language translation, in your program window. It is generally preferable to Step Over standard functions rather than to enter them.

Step Out of a Function Step Out causes the current statement indicator to exit from a function in which you currently are operating. The function will finish executing, and then you will see the current statement indicator move to the statement in the caller, just after the call to the function you just exited.

As you execute your code using the debugger, keep in mind that your primary focus should be on examining the values of critical variables and observing the program's flow of control. The overall goal, of course, is to discover points in the program where errors occur.

5.5.3 A Note on Infinite Loops

If your program contains an infinite loop, you can easily detect it using Step commands. As you step through the code, at some point you will see the program get stuck inside some loop. In this situation the current statement arrow will just keep going through the same code over and over. In this case, click on the X in the upper-right corner of your program's output window to completely halt the C++ program's execution. If that does not stop the program, try typing CTRL-ALT_DEL.

5.5.4 Using Breakpoints

Sometimes even stepping with Step Over will be too slow. You may want to run your program at normal speed up to a certain point, then stop it and check the values of critical variables at that point. *Breakpoints* are specific statement(s) at which you want your program execution to be suspended.

To the left of the main program editing window is a grey column. In this column, right click to the left of any statement in your program, and a menu will appear. Choose Insert/Remove Breakpoint from this menu. Now a small red octagon, like a stop sign, will appear next to the program line. This indicates that a breakpoint has been *set* at that statement. When you run the program now under the debugger's control, execution will automatically halt at this breakpoint.

You can insert as many breakpoints as you wish, but only in front of executable C++ statements, not at comments, declarations, and so on.

To remove a breakpoint in Visual C++, right click on the red octagon to obtain the menu again. Choose Remove Breakpoint. To remove all breakpoints in a program simultaneously, select Breakpoints from the Edit menu. Then click on Remove All.

To run a program at normal speed until a breakpoint is encountered, choose Go from the Visual C++ debugger's Debug menu. Once the program has been interrupted by a breakpoint, you can resume execution or debug using any of the commands described earlier. The Step commands may prove particularly useful once you have suspended execution at a breakpoint.

5.5.5 Changing the Value of a Variable "On the Fly"

You can answer questions such as, "What if the variable X did have the correct value of 2.3 instead of this wrong value it now has?" Again, this is accomplished by actually altering the value of the variable during the run, using the debugger. The debugger usually provides some means of doing this. In Visual C++, just double-click on the value of the variable you want to change in the variables pane. Then, type in the new value you want to use, and hit the Enter key. When you resume execution, the variable will have the value you just typed in.

5.5.6 Function Pop-Up Menus

Most IDEs provide some method of easily selecting a particular function's code to display in the program pane. For example, if the main function is currently displayed in the program window, but you want to look at function `MyFunc`, you can tell the debugger to bring `MyFunc` into the program window. In Visual C++, if you click on the small triangle displayed next to the word `main` shown above the program pane, you will see a pop-up menu of the names of the functions contained in your program, in their order of declaration. If you then select a particular function in the list, it will immediately be displayed in the program window.

5.5.7 Viewing Data Types

Data types (such as `int`, `double`, etc.) are usually not displayed alongside the names of variables in your debugger's windows; most debuggers will, however, allow you to indicate that you would like to see data types. In Visual C++, to tell the debugger to show you the data type that corresponds to a particular variable, right click on the variable name in the variables pane. Then, select Properties.

5.5.8 Displaying Values in a Structured Type Variable

The values of structured variables such as arrays, structs, and classes are typically not all displayed in the debugger's window, unless you specifically choose to have them displayed. In Visual C++, to see all of the values in a structured variable, you must click on the '+' to the left of that variable's name in the variables pane.

Note that many debuggers, as a default, will display only the memory address of the first element in a structured variable. This can be useful debugging information as well, depending on what your program needs to do.

5.5.9 Compiler and Debugger Preferences

Most compilers allow you to alter preferences that significantly affect the behavior of the debugger. In Visual C++, go to Options under the Tools menu to set your preferences.

5.6 EXAMPLE: DEBUGGING A SAMPLE C++ PROGRAM USING MICROSOFT VISUAL C++

In this section, we will look at a short, buggy C++ program. Using the interactive debugger provided in Visual C++ as an example, we will trace through the steps a programmer would go through in order to discover what is wrong in the program and then to fix it appropriately. The figures we show to illustrate the state of the debugger at various points were produced by Visual C++ and are in fact screen shots of its debugging windows. Other modern compiler systems provide similar features.

As in the CodeWarrior example, here too the C++ program we will consider is intended to repeatedly read in Fahrenheit temperatures from the user, and convert each to its equivalent Celsius value. After each temperature is converted, the user is asked whether he or she would like to convert another temperature. The process is supposed to repeat until the user indicates that he or she does not want to enter any more temperature values.

5.6.1 Sample C++ Program: Buggy Version

Consider the following initial version of the program, which produces no syntax errors or warnings:

```
#include <iostream>
using namespace std;
int main ( )
{
    int fahrenTemp, celTemp;
    char response;
    bool keepGoing = true;

    // assume user wants to do it once
    while (keepGoing)
    {
         // get a temp and convert it
         cout << "Enter a temperature in Fahrenheit -> ";
         cin >> fahrenTemp;

         celTemp = int(5/9 * (fahrenTemp - 32));
         cout << "In Celsius that is " << celTemp << endl;

         // ask if user wants to convert another
         cout << endl
              << "Do you want to enter another temperature?"
              " Enter y or n -> ";
         cin >> response;

         // input error checking
         while ((response != y) || (response != n))
         {
         cout << "Please try again. Enter y or n -> ";
         cin >> response;
         }

         // reset flag
         keepGoing = (response == y);
    }

    return 0;
}   // end of main
```

When we run this program, and observe the following output dialogue, we may begin to question our programming skills or perhaps our sanity!

```
Enter a temperature in Fahrenheit -> 75
In Celsius that is 0

Do you want to enter another temperature? Enter y or n -> y
Please try again. Enter y or n -> y
Please try again. Enter y or n -> y
Please try again. Enter y or n -> y
Please try again. Enter y or n -> n
Please try again. Enter y or n ->
```

We have to forcibly quit the program (in Visual C++, we click on the X in the upper right corner of the program's output window) in order to end this misery. We then decide to use the interactive debugger to help us figure out what's wrong. The next few sections illustrate this process.

5.6.2 Sample C++ Program: Using Step to Find the 1st Error

We see that the calculation of the Celsius temperature produces an incorrect value of 0 for a Fahrenheit value of 75. There are two critical variables here, first, `fahrenTemp`. It is possible that `fahrenTemp` is somehow not being input and stored correctly. The second critical variable is `celTemp` itself, which may not be calculated correctly. Let's check both by using the debugger to step through the program, one statement at a time, up to the point just before `celTemp's` value is output.

Figure 5.12 shows the Visual C++ debugging window just at a point after we initiated execution of the program using Step Into and then used Step Over to complete the variable declarations. In the variables pane we see the four variables we have declared, `celTemp`, `fahrenTemp`, `keepGoing` and `response`. At this point the values for all but `keepGoing` are not meaningful because the other variables are *uninitialized*. In the program pane we see our C++ source program, with the current statement indicator shown as an arrow, pointing at the next statement to be executed.

We next use the Step Over command to execute the next few lines, bringing us to the state shown in Figure 5.13. Figure 5.13 shows the current statement indicator at the output statement for `celTemp`. This means that we have already entered a value for `fahrenTemp` (75), and can check the variables pane to see if it is correct. It is correct, so `fahrenTemp` is not the problem. We next look at `celTemp`. It is 0, which we know is wrong. So we can conclude that the assignment statement which calculates `celTemp` contains some error.

Note that to interactively enter an input value for `fahrenTemp`, at the point at which you would use Step Over to execute `cin >> fahrenTemp`, you would have to click on the black button at the bottom of the screen labeled C:\, which would pull up the output window (console window) for your executing C++ program.

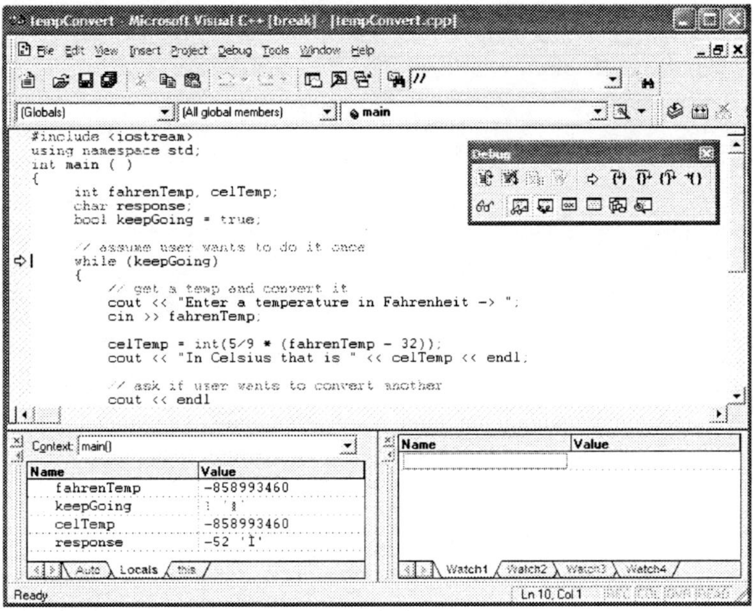

Figure 5.12

Debugging window after variable declarations completed

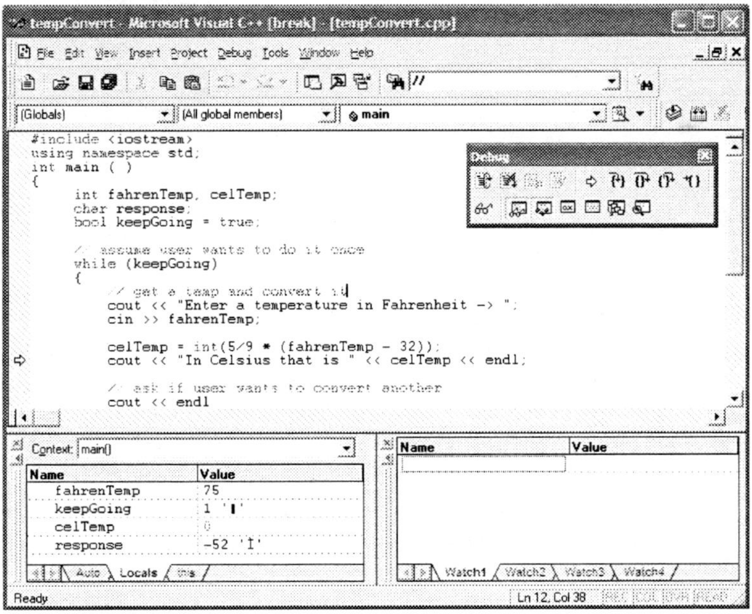

Figure 5.13

Debugging window at output line for `celTemp`, before correction

Looking at the assignment statement, we notice that while the formula looks superficially correct, the value of the expression "5/9" is zero. Because we are dividing two integer values, any fractional portion of the result would simply be truncated. That makes the value of the entire calculation zero. If we change "5/9" to evaluate using real number division, we can fix this one problem and see if we then get a correct result.

Using the Stop Debugging command, we stop execution, go back into our program code, and change the assignment statement so that it reads "5.0/9.0" instead of "5/9." Then, we start running the program again with Step Into, and use Step Over to get to the same location.

Figure 5.14 shows that we have solved our first problem. The value of `celTemp` is now 23, which is correct. We decide to Stop Debugging the program run and celebrate our first small victory. Of course, the program must be tested with other temperature values before we know it is running correctly for all possible values.

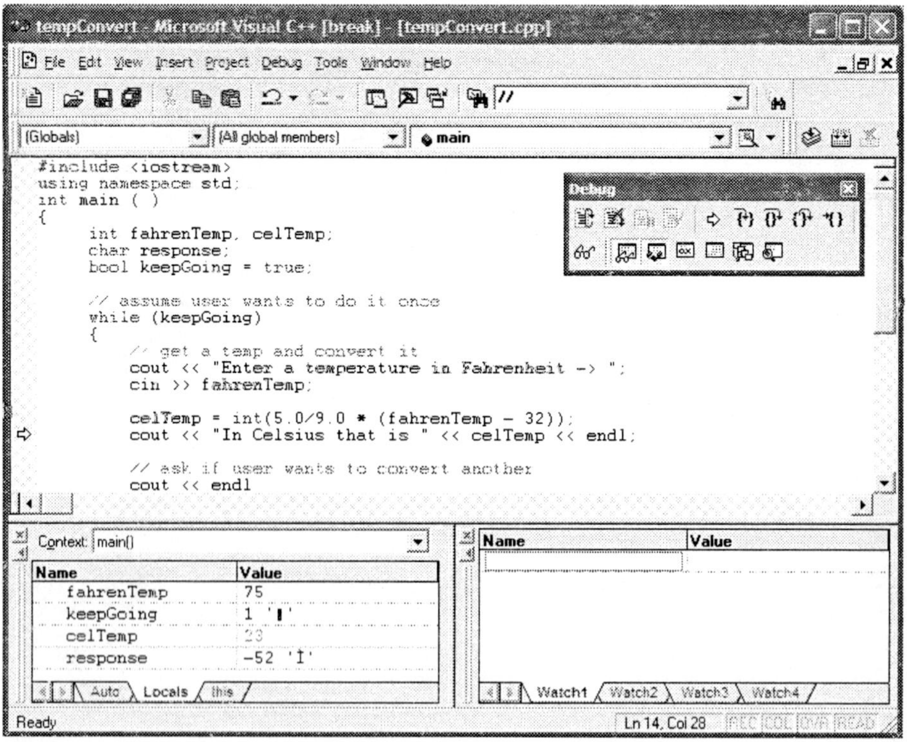

Figure 5.14

Debugging window at output line for `celTemp`, after correction

5.6.3 Sample C++ Program: Using Breakpoints to Find the 2nd Error

We can guess from our original program output that we are stuck in an *infinite loop*, the loop in which we enter a *y* or an *n* to indicate whether we want to enter another temperature or not. There is one critical variable here, `response`.

We will set breakpoints at positions that will help us determine exactly what the problem is with this loop. There are two possible reasons the loop might be infinite: (1) the input value of `response` is not being read and stored correctly, or (2) the logical expression at the loop entrance is faulty, so that even if `response` is read and stored correctly, we remain stuck.

Figure 5.15 shows the Visual C++ debugging window just at the point where we have partially executed the program, entered 75 for the Fahrenheit temperature, and chosen two breakpoints. Remember that execution will stop just before a breakpoint statement executes. Notice also that we have decided to keep a special eye on the value of response. By clicking on the variable name in its declaration to highlight it, then dragging it to the watch pane, we will make it a bit easier to notice any changes in its value.

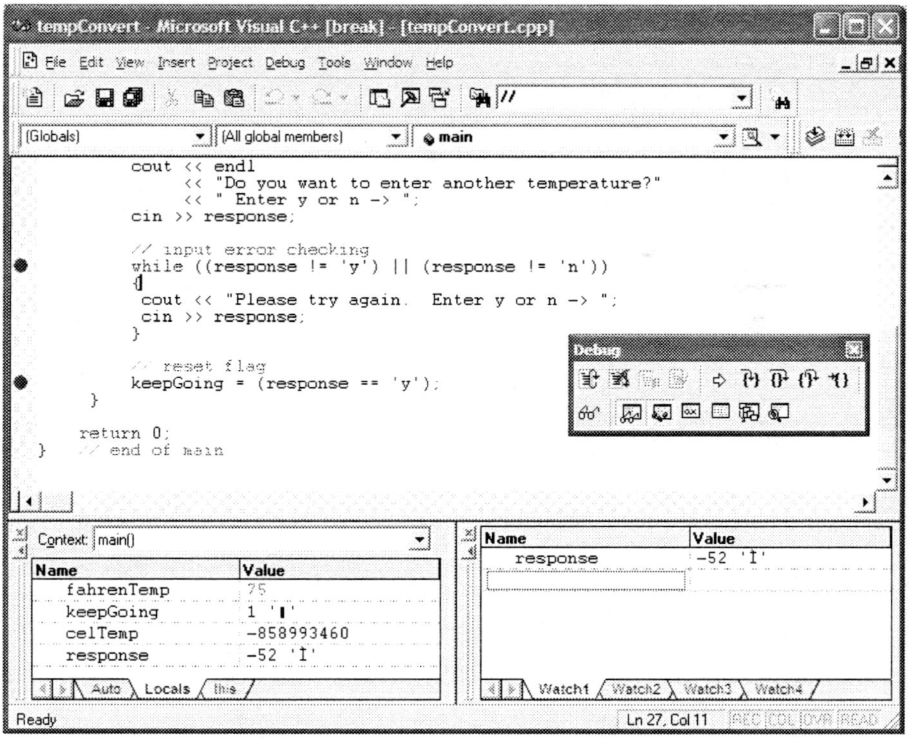

Figure 5.15

Debugging window after choosing two breakpoints

We now run the program using Go, and it stops when it hits the first breakpoint, at the top of the `while` loop we are concerned about. Figure 5.16 shows the state of the program when we have encountered this breakpoint, and then used one Step Over to find out what statement is executed next. Assume we entered a *y* when asked for a response.

Looking at the watch pane, we see that response is actually *y*, which in this case, is correct. This means `response` is being read and stored correctly. The critical variable is fine, and the loop body should not execute at all. However, the current statement indicator shows that the next statement to be executed is the `cout` call inside the loop that prints a prompt for a new value. Note that if we had correctly entered an *n*, the exact same thing would have happened. We are indeed stuck in this loop. No matter what value we type in, we will enter the loop body. We can also change the value of response "on the fly" (described earlier in this chapter) to whatever value we want to check that this is the case. We note if we tried repeatedly entering values for `response`, we would see that the current statement indicator would never reach the 2nd breakpoint that we set. The flow of control cannot get there.

Now what? The only possibility left is that the logical expression controlling the loop is wrong. Indeed, you may recall from Chapter 2 that this expression

```
(response != y) || (response != n)
```

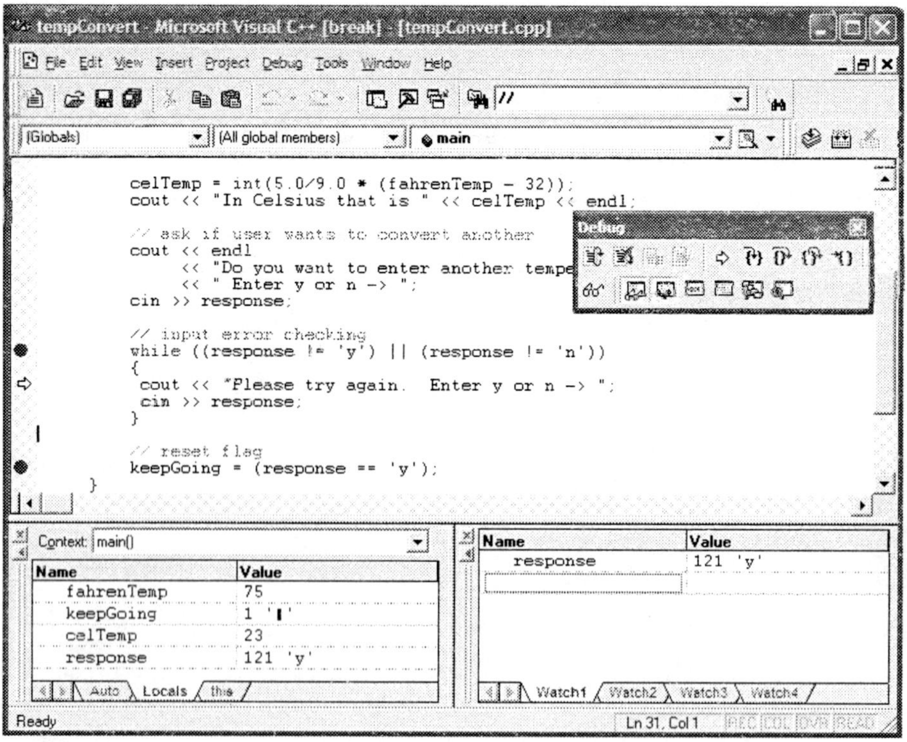

Figure 5.16

Debugging window after first breakpoint

is always true, regardless of the value of response. This is why the loop can never exit. Realizing this, we can Stop Debugging the program, change the expression to the correct version,

```
(response != y) && (response != n)
```

and run the program again. After this change, the program works correctly!

Figure 5.17 shows that once the logical expression has been corrected, the flow of control does indeed proceed to the 2nd breakpoint we set, where the variable `keepGoing` is assigned a value. We can now stop at this point, do one Step Over, and verify that `keepGoing` is being set correctly to true (1) or false (0) if we wish.

We have exited the infinite loop and successfully corrected the program. At this point it is important to continue to test the program thoroughly with different input values and input combinations, to verify that the entire program does work correctly for all possible inputs.

5.6.4 Sample C++ Program: Corrected Version

Please see section 5.4.4 for the corrected program in its entirety.

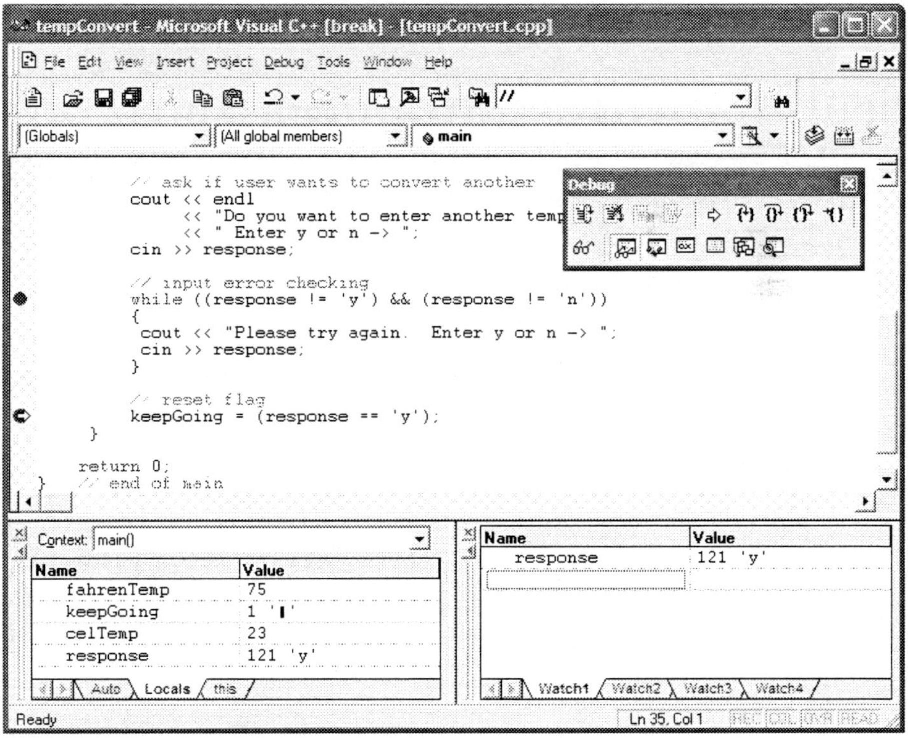

Figure 5.17

Debugging window at second breakpoint

APPENDIX A

Common Bugs in First Programs

In this appendix we summarize many of the most common bugs found in first programs based on our experience with programming classes over the past decade. This is by no means an exhaustive list, but is given as a checklist for beginning programmers to analyze their code in advance for potential bugs. More details about how to detect and correct these bugs (errors) are given in the sections in this book shown in parentheses.

1. array as a parameter handled improperly (Sec. 2.2)
2. array index out of bounds
3. call-by-value used instead of call-by-reference for function parameters to be modified
4. comparison operators misused
5. compound statement not used (Sec. 2.4)
6. dangling else (Sec. 2.4)
7. data input error (Sec. 3.2.1)
8. data output error (Sec. 3.2.2)
9. division by zero attempted
10. division using integers, so quotient gets truncated
11. files not closed properly (and thus the buffers were not flushed)
12. infinite loop (Sec. 2.4)
13 global variables used—not a bug, but bad programming practice
14. if-else not used properly
15. left hand side of assignment does not contain an L-value (Sec. 2.2)
16. loop has no body (Sec. 2.3)
17. loop termination error (Sec. 3.2.3)

18. missing "&" or missing "const" with a call-by-reference function parameter
19. missing bracket for body of function or compound statement
20. missing reference to namespace (Sec. 2.2)
21. missing return statement in a value-returning function (Sec. 2.2)
22. missing semi-colon in simple statements, function prototypes, struct definitions, or class definitions (Sec. 2.2)
23. mismatched data types in expressions.
24. operator precedence misunderstood (Sec. 2.4)
25. off-by-one error in a loop (Sec. 2.4)
26. overused (overloaded) local variable names, leading to confusion
27. pointers not set properly or overwritten in error (Sec. 4.3)
28. return with value attempted in a void function
29. switch statement error (Sec. 3.2.3)
30. undeclared variable name (Sec. 2.2)
31. uninitialized variable (Sec. 2.3)
32. unmatched parentheses (Sec. 2.2)
33. unterminated strings (Sec. 2.2)
34. using " = " when " ==" is intended (Sec. 2.3)
35. using "&" when "&&" is intended in an "if" or loop expression
36. "while" used improperly instead of "if"

A P P E N D I X B

Checklist for Error Detection and Prevention

The details of error (bug) detection and prevention methods have been very well covered by outstanding programmers and authors such as Brian Kernighan and Rob Pike in their book "The Practice of Programming" [KePi99]. Other useful ideas have appeared in books by Scott Meyers [Meye92] and Steve Maguire [Magu93] based on the Microsoft experience. Our intent here is to categorize the fundamental ideas expressed by these and other experienced programmers as a checklist for the new programmer, and hopefully lead you to read those works in depth as you progress in your programming skills.

B.1 ERROR DETECTION METHODS

Error detection methods are used to find errors that have caused the program to run incorrectly. Syntax errors will automatically be detected by your C++ compiler. Semantic errors include those that cause the program to crash or go into an infinite loop. Other semantic errors may not cause any obvious crashes or loops, but result in incorrect output. Both types of semantic errors can usually be detected with the methods given below.

1. Use the tracing method described in this book (see Chaps. 3,4) to display the value of critical variables including arrays, vectors, strings, pointers, struct members, and class members. Display them both before and after their modification in the program. The more tracing statements you put into the program, the more you can localize the problem and target in on the real error. This is often referred to as a "divide and conquer" technique.
2. Try to make the error reproducible. This will help in locating the error if you can easily reproduce its occurrence while making small changes in your

code to find the problem. Errors that are not reproducible are probably due to system or hardware errors and may not be in your code.

3. Get a stack trace of function calls to see if functions are being called in the correct sequence. This feature is usually provided as part of an interactive debugger (see Chap. 5). The debugger is a critical tool to use for error detection if simple tracing fails to find the error.
4. Once an error is found, correct it immediately while you understand what the problem is and can easily make the fix. Then check to see whether the same mistake has been made elsewhere and fix those occurrences immediately.
5. Examine the most recent code change. Very often, corrections to errors contain new errors, so it is useful to carefully check all changes just made.

B.2 WHERE TO INSERT TRACES AND WHAT VARIABLES TO DISPLAY

In this section we summarize with some rules of thumb about where to insert the traces into the program code and what variables to display for each type of trace. Think of this as a checklist that can be added to or subtracted from, depending on the specific conditions in your program code.

1. **Sequential code (no control statements)**
   - display critical variables at the end of each 10-15 lines of purely sequential code.

2. **if-else statements**
   - display critical variables just before and after if and else conditions

3. **while and for loops**
   - display critical variables just before and after while or for blocks
   - display critical variables within while or for loops consistently just before or after the increment or decrement of the loop counter.
   - display the loop counter

4. **Functions**
   - display all parameters before and after each function entry
   - display all parameters before and after each function exit

5. **Arrays**
   - display array components and array index values

6. **Character strings**
   - display critical variables before and after each use of a string function.

7. **Structs and class objects**
   - display critical variables in a struct or class object just after initialization and any update, including updates from constructors

8. Pointers

- display pointer values before and after each update of a pointer. Pointer addresses may not be meaningful at first, but keep track of them for comparative purposes to make sure the values are not corrupted during the program execution.

B.3 ERROR PREVENTION AND TESTING METHODS

1. Use good design techniques, good programming style (use indentation, do not use global variables, etc.), and well-designed interfaces among functions and with the user.
2. Study your code thoroughly before typing it in or before running it. This is often referred to as a *code inspection* or*walkthrough*. Explain your code to someone else if possible, ideally to another programmer you are working with, as part of the walkthrough.
3. Make your program self-documented with comments to describe the definitions of all variables, the purpose of functions and interfaces to functions, and a brief description of the purpose of each control structure (loop, selection statement, or function).
4. Insert assertions and self-checking code to test for the possibility of bad input data to the program, and protect the program from crashing with bad data. This is also referred to as *defensive programming*.
5. Test your code at the boundary values for variables and for pre- and post-conditions. This involves tracing variables used just before and after control structures are entered (selection statements "if" and "switch," looping statements "while", "do while", and "for," and function calls), tracing of values used inside these control structures including testing the execution of each branch in selection statements, and testing "for" and "while" loops so the loop indexes are properly set before the loop executes and when it finishes. This technique can also be used to avoid the division-by-zero problem.
6. Avoid the error recurrence problem by keeping a log of all bugs fixed.
7. Test your program incrementally, after each function is written, or subdivide a function into parts that can be tested independently. Don't wait until you have ALL the code written before doing any testing. By then, the errors will be much harder to localize and detect.
8. Consider these behavioral properties in all programs:

   - *correctness*—does the program produce correct output for correct input?
   - *reliability* (robustness)—does the program handle incorrect data properly?
   - *utility*—is the program easy to use?
   - *performance*—is the program efficient, that is, does it execute quickly enough to satisfy the needs of the user of the program?

Bibliography

[Bugg98] Bugg, K. Debugging C++ Windows , R & D Books, 1998.

[Dale02] Dale, N.B., Weems, C., and Headington, M. Programming and Problem Solving with C++, 3rd Edition, Jones and Bartlett Pub., 2002.

[Deit05] Deitel, H.M. and Deitel, P.J. C++ How to Program, 5th Edition, Prentice Hall, 2005.

[Kern99] Kernighan, B.W. and Pike, R. The Practice of Programming , Addison-Wesley, 1999.

[Lenc00] Lencevicius, R. Advanced Debugging Methods , Kluwer Academic Publishing, 2000.

[Magu93] Maguire, S. Writing Solid Code , Microsoft Press, 1993.

[McCo93] McConnell, S. Code Complete , Microsoft Press, 1993.

[Meye92] Meyers, S. Effective C++, Addison-Wesley, 1992.

[Papp00] Pappas, C.H. and Murray, W.H. III Debugging C++: Troubleshooting for Programmers , McGraw-Hill, 2000.

[Robb00] Robbins, J. Debugging Applications , Microsoft Press, 2000.

[Rose00] Rosenberg, J.B. How Debuggers Work: Algorithms, Data Structures, and Architecture, Wiley, 1996.

[Savi04] Savitch, W. Problem Solving With C++: The Object of Programming, 5th Edition, Addison Wesley, 2004.

[Stit92] Stitt, M. Debugging: Creative Techniques and Tools for Software Repair , Wiley, 1992.

Index